# Energy, Light, & Sound

## Grades 1–3

INVESTIGATING SCIENCE

**Project Managers:**
Karen A. Brudnak, Thad H. McLaurin

**Writers:**
Valerie Wood Smith, Laura Wagner

**Editors:**
Cindy K. Daoust, Scott Lyons, Leanne Stratton, Hope H. Taylor

**Art Coordinator:**
Clevell Harris

**Artists:**
Theresa Lewis Goode, Clevell Harris,
Rob Mayworth, Donna K. Teal

**Cover Artists:**
Nick Greenwood, Kimberly Richard

**www.themailbox.com**

©2000 by THE EDUCATION CENTER, INC.
All rights reserved.
ISBN #1-56234-429-3

Manufactured in the United States

10  9  8  7  6  5  4  3  2

# Table of Contents

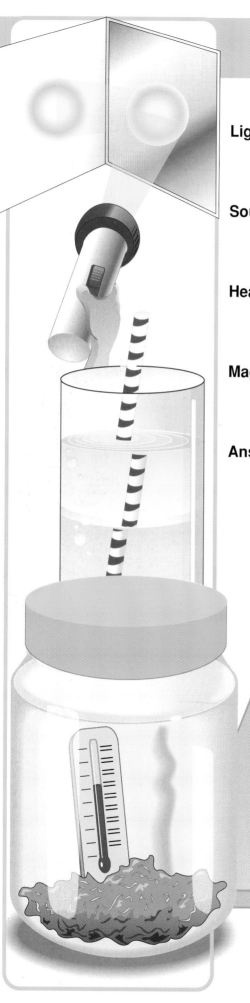

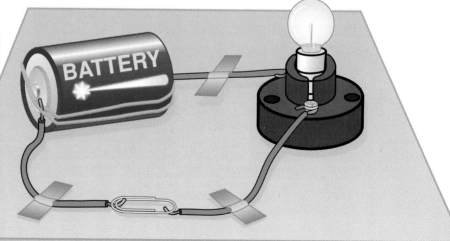

# About This Book

Welcome to *Investigating Science—Energy, Light, & Sound*! This book is one of ten must-have resource books that support the National Science Education Standards and are designed to supplement and enhance your existing science curriculum. Packed with practical cross-curricular ideas and thought-provoking reproducibles, these all-new, content-specific resource books provide primary teachers with a collection of innovative and fun activities for teaching thematic science units.

### Included in this book:

*Investigating Science—Energy, Light, & Sound* contains four cross-curricular thematic units each containing
- Background information for the teacher
- Easy-to-implement instructions for science experiments and projects
- Student-centered activities and reproducibles
- Literature links

### Cross-curricular thematic units found in this book:
- *Light*
- *Sound*
- *Heat*
- *Magnetism and Electricity*

### Other books in the primary Investigating Science series:
- *Investigating Science—Amphibians & Reptiles*
- *Investigating Science—Environment*
- *Investigating Science—Solar System*
- *Investigating Science—Mammals*
- *Investigating Science—Insects*
- *Investigating Science—Plants*
- *Investigating Science—Weather*
- *Investigating Science—Rocks & Minerals*
- *Investigating Science—Health & Safety*

Scientific Facts "...ap" the World
- Light is a form of energy made up of electric and magnetic fields and is called an *electromagnetic wave*.
- ...al light ...main source of ...reen plants use...rth. ...ood-making proc...ght in the *photosynthesis*. ...s called
- Light travels in stra...ght lines. ...ght rays *reflect*... ...some object...m, or b...unce
- Lig... ...be *refracted*, or bent.
- *Shadows* are formed... objects block the ligh...
- Objects can be categ... *transparent, translu...opaque*, depending...amount of light able...through them.

# Light

*Enlighten and entertain your youngsters with this collection of fun activities, ideas, and reproducibles on light—a source of energy on which we all depend!*

## Right to the Source
### (Identifying Light Sources, Making a Booklet)

When a lonely firefly searches for a friend, he encounters many sources of light before he finds the companions he seeks. Share *The Very Lonely Firefly* by Eric Carle (The Putnam Publishing Group, 1995) with the class. During a rereading of the book, have the students identify all of the light sources mentioned and list these on a sheet of chart paper. Then encourage students to brainstorm other sources of light to add to the list. Follow up by guiding each child through the following steps to make his own light source booklet.

**Materials needed for each child:**
1 copy of page 10
one 4" square of yellow construction paper
scissors
Crayola® Construction Paper™ crayons
access to a stapler

**Directions:**
1. Cut out the six booklet pages on page 10.
2. Carefully cut out the white circles on booklet pages 1–5. (This may need to be done in advance for younger students.)
3. Stack the booklet pages in numerical order. Place the stack on top of the yellow piece of construction paper. Line up the top edge of the stack with the top edge of the yellow paper and staple the booklet at the top. Trim off the excess yellow paper at the bottom and sides of the stack.
4. Use Crayola® Construction Paper™ crayons to turn the visible yellow circle on each booklet page into an illustration of a different light source from the brainstormed list.
5. Write the name of each light source below each illustration.
6. Color the title and Sun on the booklet's title page and write your name on the line.

## Background for the Teacher
- Light is a form of energy made up of electric and magnetic fields and is called an *electromagnetic wave.*
- The Sun is the main source of natural light for Earth.
- Green plants use light in the food-making process called *photosynthesis.*
- Light travels in straight lines.
- Light rays *reflect* from, or bounce off, some objects.
- Light rays can be *refracted,* or bent.
- *Shadows* are formed when objects block the light.
- Objects can be categorized as *transparent, translucent,* or *opaque,* depending on the amount of light able to shine through them.
- The primary colors of *white light* are red, blue, and green.
- Rainbows are formed when water droplets act as prisms and split the sunlight into the separate rainbow colors.

## Illuminating Literature
*Light and Sight* (Science Factory) by Jon Richards (Copper Beech Books, 1999)

*The Magic School Bus® Gets a Bright Idea: A Book About Light* by Joanna Cole (Scholastic Inc., 1997)

*The Magic School Bus® Makes a Rainbow: A Book About Color* by Joanna Cole (Scholastic Inc., 1997)

*Shadows and Reflections* by Tana Hoban (Greenwillow Books, 1990)

*Sound and Light* (Young Discoverers series) by David Glover (Kingfisher, 1993)

*What Makes a Shadow?* (Let's-Read-and-Find-Out Science) by Clyde Robert Bulla (HarperCollins Children's Books, 1994)

# Two Types of Light
## (Classification, Making a Journal)

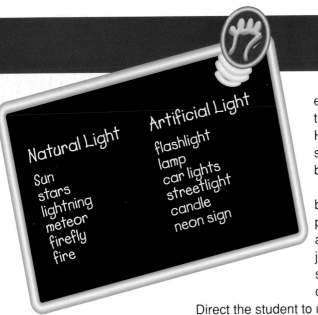

Natural Light

Sun
stars
lightning
meteor
firefly
fire

Artificial Light

flashlight
lamp
car lights
streetlight
candle
neon sign

Use the following activity to shed a little light on the two different types of light sources. Explain to your students that the two types of light sources are *natural* and *artificial,* or man-made. Help students to better understand this concept by having each student make a journal of the light sources she sees. Begin by brainstorming a list for each type of light (see the sample list).

Next, give each child one construction paper copy of the light-bulb pattern at the top of page 11, five copies of the lightbulb pattern at the bottom of page 11, scissors, markers or crayons, and access to a stapler. Instruct each student to cut out the journal cover, personalize it, and decorate it as desired. Have the student cut out the other five pages and stack them, place the cover on top, and staple it all together at the top.

Direct the student to use the journal to keep a record of the different light sources she sees over a period of five days. Have her draw each light source on a separate journal page, write its name, and then label the source either "natural" or "artificial" by checking the appropriate box. Make available extra patterns for students who may need to add pages to their journals. At the end of five days, have each child share her findings with the class.

# The Path of Light
## (Demonstration)

Five index cards, a hole puncher, a piece of modeling clay, a flashlight, and some talcum powder are the only props you'll need to demonstrate for your students that light travels in a straight line. Hole-punch the center of four of the index cards. Place four small balls of clay about four inches apart in a straight line on a table. Next, stand a hole-punched card in each ball of clay so that the holes are lined up exactly as shown. Use a small ball of clay to place the fifth index card at the end of the row.

Darken the room and direct the beam of the flashlight through the hole in the front card. Ask a student volunteer to sprinkle a small amount of talcum powder over the beam so that it is clearly visible. Lead students in a discussion of their observations of the beam. *(The flashlight's beam travels in a straight path through the holes to reflect off the fifth card.)* Have student volunteers predict what will happen if one of the cards is moved slightly to the left or right. Then move one of the cards slightly and shine the beam through the first card again. *(Because light travels in a straight line, when the holes are no longer lined up, the beam will not reach the fifth card.)*

# Polka-Dot Gardens
## (Experiment)

Amaze and educate your youngsters about the power of light by having them grow polka-dot gardens! Inform your students that light provides the necessary energy plants need to grow. Next, divide the class into small groups. Provide each group with the following materials; then guide each group through the directions below to see how light and the lack of light affects plant growth.

**Materials needed for each group:**

flat, rectangular pan or baking dish
cotton balls
alfalfa seeds
sheet of poster board slightly larger than the surface of the pan

scissors
water
tape

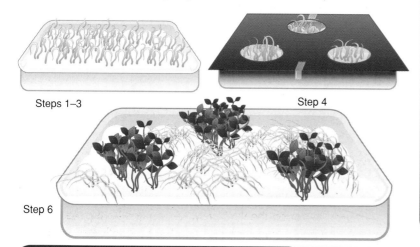

Steps 1–3

Step 4

Step 6

**Directions:**

1. Cover the bottom of the pan with cotton balls.
2. Moisten the cotton balls; then sprinkle the seeds over them.
3. Place the pan in a sunny window. Keep the cotton balls moist until the seeds have sprouted (about four days).
4. Cut out of the poster board three or four small circles several inches apart as shown. On the fourth day, place the poster board on top of the pan and secure in place with tape. Continue to keep the cotton balls moist. (After watering, it is important to replace the poster board in the exact same position over the pan.)
5. After ten days, remove the poster board and examine the seedlings. Record your observations. *(The seedlings underneath the circular cutouts will appear greener and thicker.)*
6. After 20 days, remove the poster board and examine the plants. Record your findings.
7. Explain the outcome of the experiment. *(The seedlings under the circular cutouts were able to use the light to produce the needed energy/food to grow. The seedlings not exposed to light died because they could not produce the needed energy/food to grow.)*

## Possible Objects for Testing

paper plates
lenses from sunglasses
waxed paper
tissue paper
different types of
  cups and glasses

plastic wrap
wrapping paper
aluminum foil
colored water

# Oh Say, Can You See Through?
## (Demonstration, Experiment)

Use the following activity to lead students to discover that objects can be classified as *transparent, translucent,* or *opaque* according to the amount of light they let pass through them. Place three empty clear plastic bottles on a table. Fill bottle #1 with water, fill bottle #2 with a mixture of half milk and half water, and cover bottle #3 with black paper. Shine a flashlight on the back of each bottle while students observe the front of each bottle. Ask students to identify the bottle through which light can clearly be seen *(bottle #1)*. Tell students that the clear water is *transparent,* allowing a lot of light to pass through the bottle. Next, have your students identify the bottle through which light can be seen but not clearly *(bottle #2)*. Inform your youngsters that the milky water is *translucent,* allowing some light to pass through the bottle. Then have students identify the bottle through which no light can be seen *(bottle #3)*. Explain that the paper is *opaque,* allowing no light to pass through the bottle.

Next, pair students and provide each pair with one copy of page 12, a flashlight, and a variety of transparent, translucent, and opaque objects (see list). Instruct each pair to choose an object and draw a picture of it in the box labeled "Object 1" on page 12. Next, have the pair predict whether the object is transparent, translucent, or opaque. Then have the pair shine the flashlight on the object to test its prediction. Direct the pair to write the test results on the line provided. Have the pair repeat the process with the remaining objects. Allow time for students to share their results with the class.

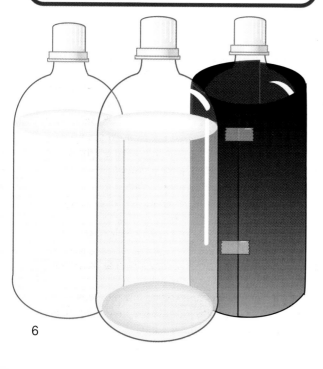

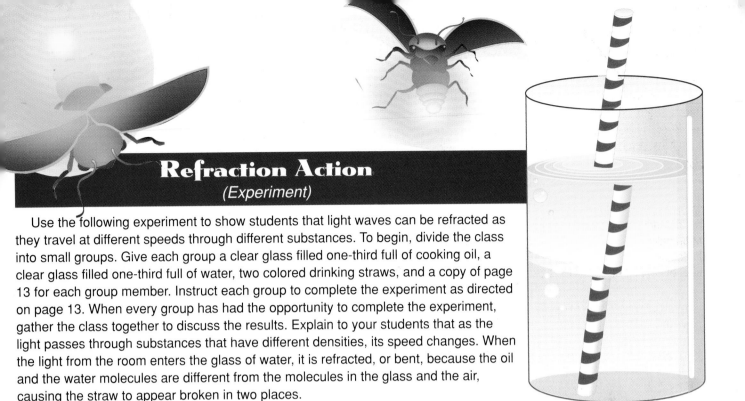

# Refraction Action
## (Experiment)

Use the following experiment to show students that light waves can be refracted as they travel at different speeds through different substances. To begin, divide the class into small groups. Give each group a clear glass filled one-third full of cooking oil, a clear glass filled one-third full of water, two colored drinking straws, and a copy of page 13 for each group member. Instruct each group to complete the experiment as directed on page 13. When every group has had the opportunity to complete the experiment, gather the class together to discuss the results. Explain to your students that as the light passes through substances that have different densities, its speed changes. When the light from the room enters the glass of water, it is refracted, or bent, because the oil and the water molecules are different from the molecules in the glass and the air, causing the straw to appear broken in two places.

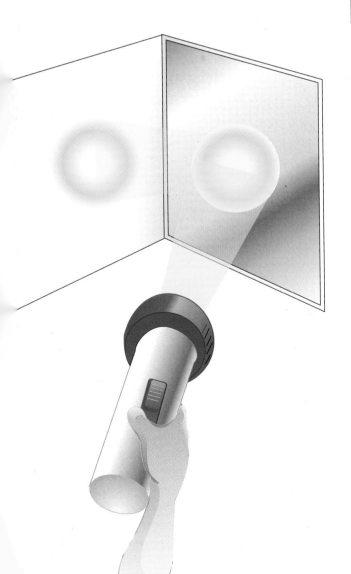

# Mirror, Mirror on the Wall
## (Experiment, Making Predictions)

Mirror, mirror on the wall, what reflects the best of all? Have students work in small groups to perform the following experiment to determine the characteristics of a reflective surface. To begin, supply each group with the materials listed; then guide each group through the steps listed.

**Materials needed for each group:**
flashlight
9" x 12" sheet of white construction paper
several testing surfaces, including a mirror, waxed paper, aluminum foil, fabric, a paper towel, a piece of Plexiglas®, a piece of wood, and other assorted surfaces

**Directions:**
1. As a group, predict which testing surface is the most reflective; then follow Steps 2–4 to test your prediction.
2. Have one group member hold the white paper at a right angle against the mirror.
3. Instruct a second group member to direct the flashlight's beam into the mirror while holding the flashlight close to the mirror. Direct her to adjust the angle of the beam until the light is reflected from the mirror onto the sheet of paper.
4. Rank the test surface using the following scale:

| 1 | 2 | 3 | 4 | 5 |
|---|---|---|---|---|
| Not Reflective | | Reflective | | Very Reflective |

5. Repeat the experiment replacing the mirror with another test surface. Rank the test surface's reflectivity.
6. Repeat the experiment with the remaining test surfaces.
7. Compare the rankings of the test surfaces to determine which surfaces were the most reflective.

7

# Jiggly Lenses
## (Experiment)

Playing with your food has never been more educational! Have your students create gelatin lenses to help them better understand how lenses refract light, making things look nearer or bigger. After students have experimented with the various Jell-O® lenses they've created, explain to them that the curved surface of the lens refracts the light that is passing through it. When the light is refracted, the words on the page appear to be larger.

### Materials needed:
one 3-ounce box of yellow or orange Jell-O®
hot water
several different kitchen utensils and/or containers with curved
    bottoms such as measuring spoons, ladles, ice-cream scoops, or
    dessert goblets
nonstick cooking spray
mixing bowl
spoon
1-cup measuring cup
large flat baking dish half-filled with uncooked rice
several small pieces of clear Plexiglas®; flat, clear lids;
    or flat, clear glass plates
access to a refrigerator
newspaper and/or magazines

### Directions:
1. Stir the Jell-O and one cup of hot water in the mixing bowl until the Jell-O is dissolved.
2. Lightly coat the insides of the curved containers with nonstick cooking spray.
3. Place the curved containers in the dish of rice to keep them from tipping. Carefully pour Jell-O into each container.
4. Place the baking dish in the refrigerator for approximately three hours or until the Jell-O sets.
5. To remove each lens from its container, place it upside down on a piece of Plexiglas, a clear plastic lid, or a clear glass plate and gently tap the bottom of the container. If it doesn't come out, place the container in a dish of hot water for ten seconds; then try again. If needed, repeat the hot water step until the lens slides out of the container.
6. Place the Plexiglas, lid, or plate containing a lens on top of a sheet of newspaper or a magazine page. Lift and adjust the lens to view the magnified page. View the same page with the various lenses and compare which has the best magnification.

## Scientific Facts "Light-up" the World

- Light is a form of energy made up of electric and magnetic fields and is called an *electromagnetic wave.*
- [Na]tural light [is the] main source of [light on the] earth.
- [G]reen plants u[se] [li]ght in the [f]ood-making pro[cess] called [p]hotosynthesis.
- [Light travels in] straight line[s]. [Li]ght travels i[n a strai]ght [path], or b[o]unce[s]. [Light] rays ref[lect].
- Ligh[t can] be *refrac[t]ed,* or bent.
- *Shadows* are formed when objects block the light.
- Objects can be categorized as *transparent, translucent,* or *opaque,* depending on the amount of light able to shine through them.

## Ouch! That's Hot!
### (Demonstration)

How much heat does a lightbulb create? Have your youngsters try this simple experiment to find out! Record the temperature from an outdoor thermometer. Then tape the thermometer to a white sheet of paper. Place the sheet of paper on the floor. Have student volunteers take turns holding an exposed, lit, clear incandescent lightbulb approximately two inches above the thermometer. (Remind students not to look directly at the bulb or touch it.) Have a different student read and record the temperature every 4 minutes for 12 minutes. Discuss the results of the experiment with the class. *(The temperature rises.)* Then have students predict what might happen if they move the lightbulb four inches away from the thermometer, then six inches from the thermometer. If desired, repeat the experiment, placing the lightbulb four inches and then six inches from the thermometer to test your students' predictions.

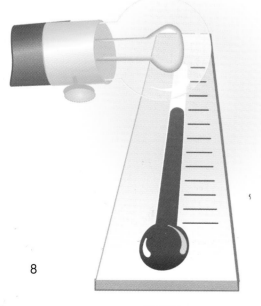

8

# Spin It!
## (Experiment, Art)

Mesmerize your students by having them each make a magic color wheel! Before making the wheels, inform your students that Sir Isaac Newton, a scientist who lived over 300 years ago, discovered that sunlight is actually made of many different colors: red, orange, yellow, green, blue, indigo (a bluish purple), and violet. Further explain that these colors form a band called a *spectrum.* Hold up a red apple and tell your students that they see the color red because the apple is reflecting the red light while it absorbs the other colors of the spectrum. Then supply each student with the materials listed and guide them through the steps below to see how the colors of the spectrum create *white light.*

**Materials for each student:** crayons or markers (red, orange, yellow, green, blue, violet), scissors, glue, one 2' length of string, 1 copy of the patterns at the bottom of this page

**Directions:**
1. Color each section of the circles below as labeled.
2. Cut out both circles.
3. Align the center holes. Then glue the circles together so that the colored side is showing on both circles. Use the tip of the scissors to poke a hole into each of the two smaller center holes.
4. Insert the two-foot string up through one hole, then down through the other hole. Tie the ends together to create a big loop.
5. Loop one end of the string over each index finger. Then flip the circle over and over until the string is twisted very tightly.
6. To make the circle spin, evenly pull your hands apart. As the circle begins to slow, move your hands inward; then pull them outward again. Repeat this process to keep the circle spinning.
7. Look at the spinning circle. What happens to the colors? *(The colors blend into a creamy color because your eye cannot detect individual colors at this speed.)*

**Note:** If the circles were divided into seven equal sections and all the colors of the spectrum were used, including *indigo,* you would see pure *white light* as you spin the circle.

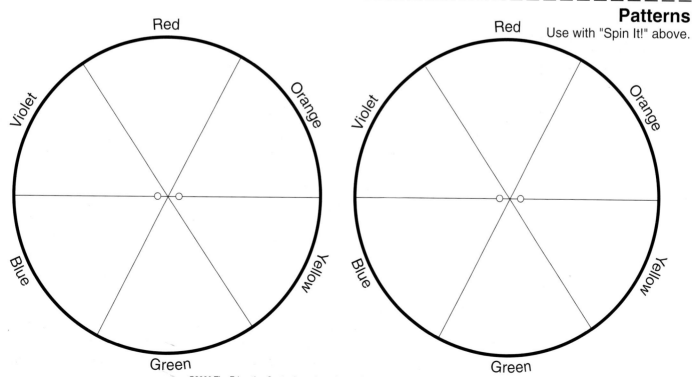

## Patterns
Use with "Spin It!" above.

Red · Orange · Yellow · Green · Blue · Violet

# Booklet Project

Use with "Right to the Source" on page 4.

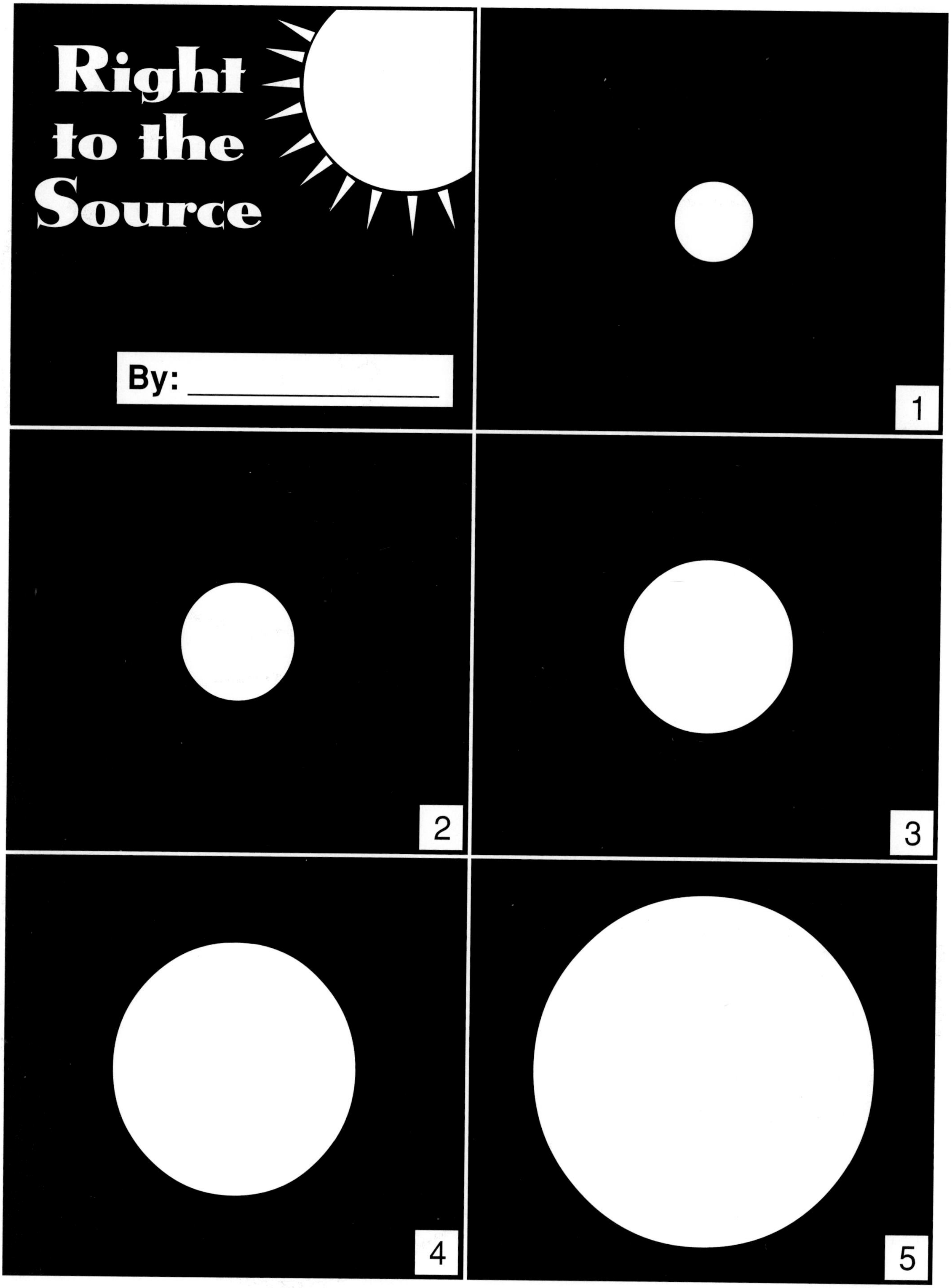

**Right to the Source**

By: _____

1

2

3

4

5

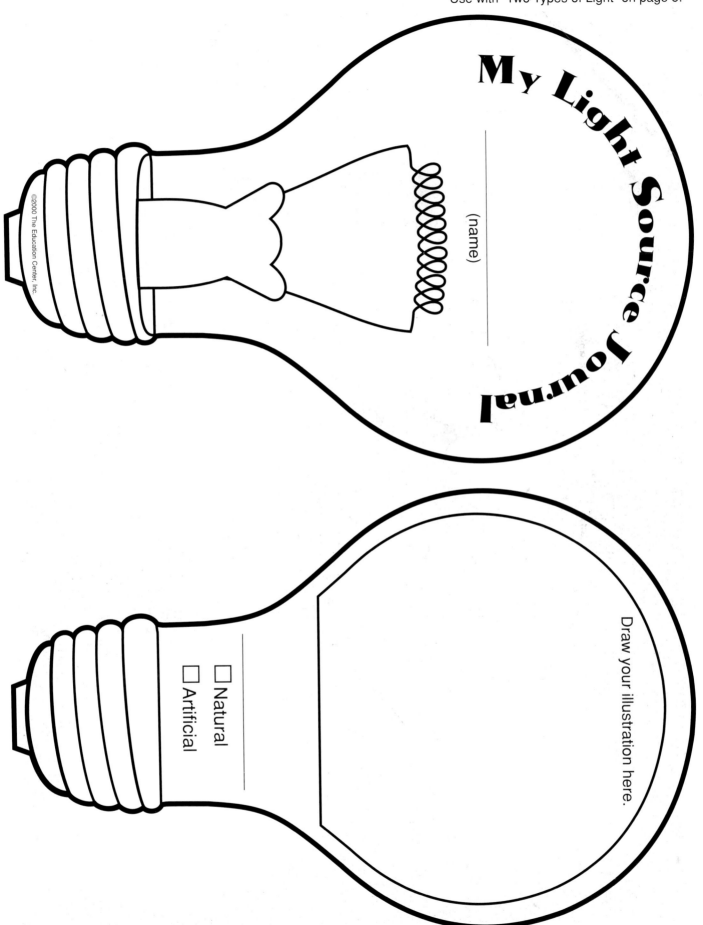

My Light Source Journal

(name)

©2000 The Education Center, Inc.

☐ Natural
☐ Artificial

Draw your illustration here.

Names _____ *Experiment*

## Object 1

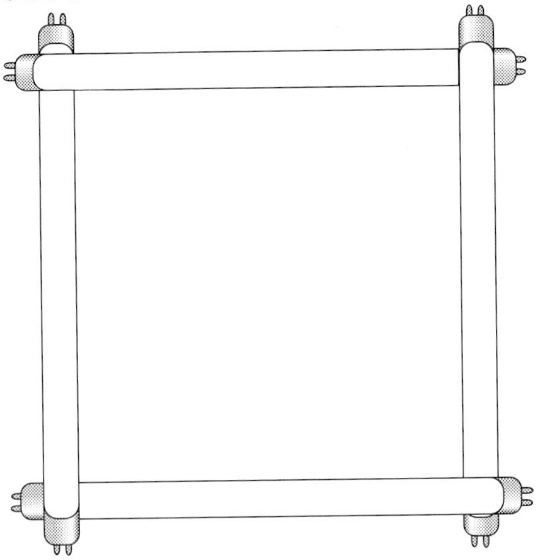

**Prediction:**
I think this object is…
- ☐ opaque
- ☐ translucent
- ☐ transparent

**Results:**
This object is _____.

## Object 2

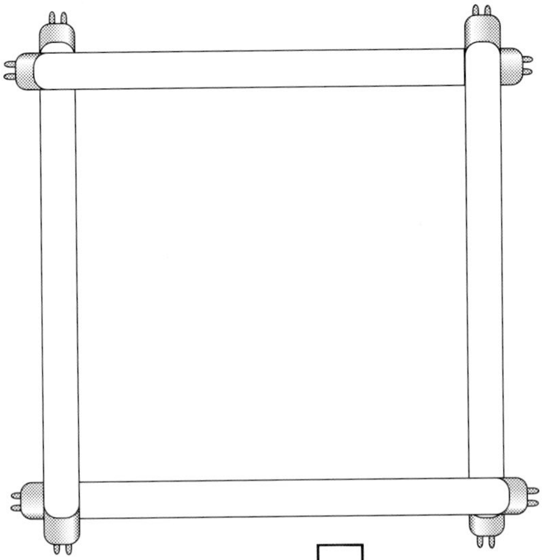

**Prediction:**
I think this object is…
- ☐ opaque
- ☐ translucent
- ☐ transparent

**Results:**
This object is _____.

## Object 3

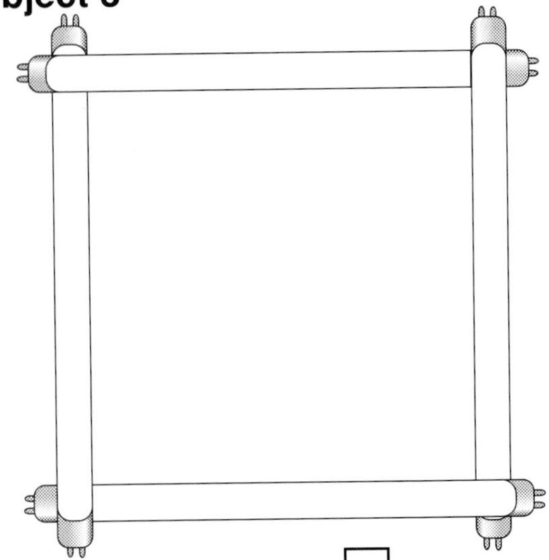

**Prediction:**
I think this object is…
- ☐ opaque
- ☐ translucent
- ☐ transparent

**Results:**
This object is _____.

## Object 4

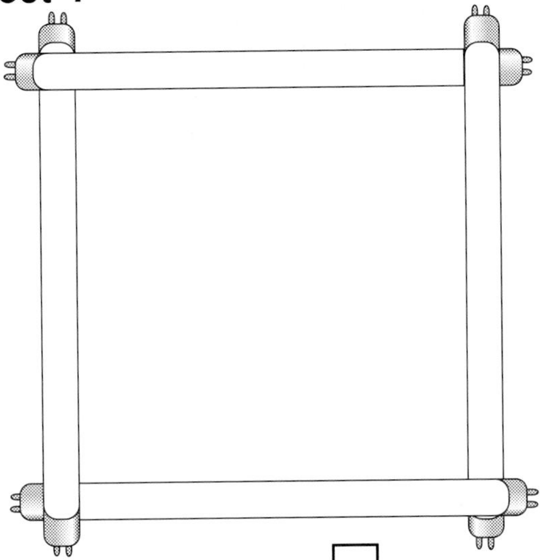

**Prediction:**
I think this object is…
- ☐ opaque
- ☐ translucent
- ☐ transparent

**Results:**
This object is _____.

**Note to the teacher:** Use with "Oh Say, Can You See Through?" on page 6.

# Refraction Action

1. Draw a picture of the glass of water and the glass of oil.

2. Place a straw in the glass of water. Look at the straw from all angles. Then draw a picture of the straw as it looks while facing the glass.

3. Place a straw in the glass of oil. Look at the straw from all angles. Then draw a picture of the straw as it looks while facing the glass.

4. Gently pour the oil into the glass of water. Wait a few seconds for all the oil to settle on top of the water. Draw a picture of the straw as it looks while facing the glass.

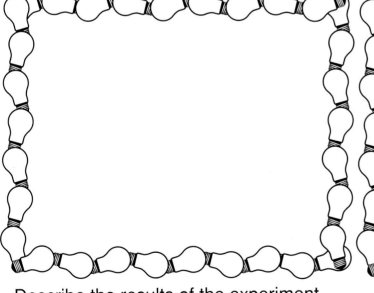

Describe the results of the experiment.

_____

_____

# Sound

Now hear this! Get your students' attention as they investigate the highs and lows of sound with these fun activities and experiments.

## Background for the Teacher

- Sound is made by *vibrations*.
- Sound travels in waves.
- Energy from vibrations stirs up surrounding air molecules, allowing the sound wave to spread out away from the source of the vibration.
- Sound waves can move through solids, liquids, and gases.
- Sound is absent in outer space.
- Echoes are sound waves that are reflected, or bounce back, from an object such as a wall to your ears.
- *Pitch* is the highness or lowness of a sound as perceived by a listener.
- The human voice is produced in the *larynx* (located in the throat), which has folds of tissue called *vocal cords*.
- Almost all mammals have vocal cords or similar structures to make sounds.
- Musical sounds are usually pleasing sounds to the ear.
- Noise is an unpleasant sound that is produced by irregular vibrations at irregular intervals.
- Sound waves enter the ear and are changed into nerve signals, which are then interpreted as sounds by the brain.
- Sound moves through the air at a rate of 1,115 feet (340 meters) per second.

## Sound Sense
*(Identifying Sounds, Listening)*

Perk your students' listening skills with the following sensory activity. In advance, tape-record a variety of indoor and outdoor sounds (such as a doorbell, a phone ringing, pots clanging, a car horn, a lawn mower, etc.). Instruct students to close their eyes and listen to the tape recording without talking. Then ask students to identify the sounds they remember hearing as you record their responses on a chart. Play the tape recording again and compare the actual sounds with those listed on the chart. Guide your students in correctly identifying each sound. Have your students discuss why some sounds were more difficult to recognize than others. (Some sounds are difficult to recognize without seeing the context in which the sounds are being made.) Encourage students to tape-record sounds at home (with a parent/guardian's permission). Then allow students to play a few of the recorded sounds for classmates to guess.

## Sound Literature

*Hey, What's That Sound?* by Veronika Martenova Charles (Stoddart Kids, 1997)

*The Listening Walk* by Paul Showers (HarperCollins Children's Books, 1991)

*The Science Book of Sound* by Neil Ardley (Harcourt Brace & Company, 1991)

*Sound and Light* (Young Discoverers Series) by David Glover (Kingfisher Books, 1993)

*The Very Noisy Night* by Diana Hendry (Dutton Children's Books, 1999)

Play this sound-matching game and improve students' listening skills too! In advance, program pairs of cards with animal pictures or names. Explain to students that birds, frogs, and almost all mammals have vocal cords or similar structures to make sounds. Instruct students to remain quiet until all the cards have been distributed. Then give each child a card and ask him to move around the classroom as he imitates the sound of the animal on his card. The goal is for each pair of animals to find each other by searching for a similar sound. Challenge students' sound-making abilities by adding a descriptor to each animal card (for example an angry bear, a hungry kitten, or an injured lion). Your students will have a roaring good time!

# Virtuoso Vocalist
## (Simulation)

Encourage your students to raise their voices with this *vocal cord* simulation. Explain to students that the human voice is produced in a section of the throat called the *larynx,* or voice box. Explain to your students that the larynx is covered with two small folds of skin called vocal cords. Further explain that as air rushes from the lungs over the vocal cords, it causes them to vibrate, producing sounds. To simulate the action of the vocal cords, give each student a balloon and ask him to inflate it. Instruct students to hold the neck of the balloon firmly between the thumb and index finger of each hand. Then have each student produce different sounds by stretching the balloon opening and slowly releasing air from the balloon. Explain to your students that the air-filled balloon is similar to their lungs, which push air past the vocal cords (similar to the neck of the balloon), creating sounds. Then ask each student to place his hand on his throat at his Adam's apple while making sounds. Tell students that the vibrations they feel come from their tightened vocal cords.

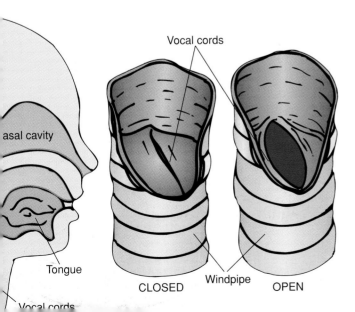

Vocal cords

Nasal cavity

Tongue

CLOSED    Windpipe    OPEN

Vocal cords

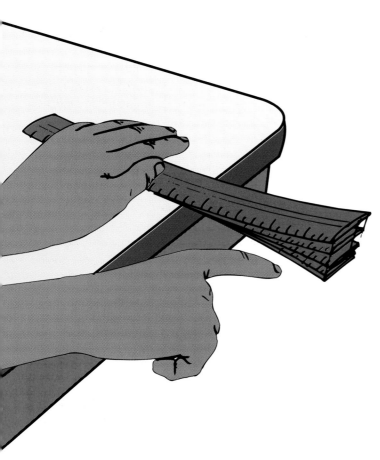

Focus on the ups and downs of sound with this refreshing investigation. To prepare, ask each student to bring a can of soda or juice to school. Explain to students that the *pitch* of a sound is determined by how rapidly an object vibrates. To begin, divide your students into small groups equipped with their canned beverages and pencils. First, instruct each group member to drink a different amount of beverage so that each group will have a range of liquid levels in their cans. Have one student at a time tap his can with a pencil as the rest of his group listens to the sound it creates. Then ask each group to compare the sound made by each can and decide if it has a high-pitched sound or a low-pitched sound. Have groups place their cans in order from lowest sound to highest. Explain to students that sound is produced by the vibrating can, and the amount of liquid in each can affects the rate of vibration. So the cans with more liquid vibrate slower, which produces low-pitched sounds, and the cans with less liquid vibrate faster, which produces high-pitched sounds.

# Sound in Motion
## (Vibration Experiment)

Help your students view vibrations with this quick and easy experiment. Explain to your students that all sounds are produced by *vibrations* or the rapid back-and-forth movement of an object. Instruct each student to place a plastic ruler on the edge of a desk and hold it firmly with one hand. Use the other hand to carefully bend the ruler down and let it go. Ask students to observe the ruler's vibrations and listen to the sound it produces. Then instruct students to slide the ruler back onto the desk so that less of the ruler hangs off the edge and repeat the process. Have your students compare the difference in frequency of vibration and pitch, or highness or lowness of sound, between the two experiments. Guide students to realize that the shorter length of ruler protruding over the desk edge produces quicker vibrations and higher sounds.

# Riding the Sound Wave
## (Simulation)

Your students will enjoy catching a wave with these simple simulation activities. Explain to students that a sound wave occurs when a vibrating object causes the surrounding solid, liquid, or gas to vibrate, creating a series of back-and-forth movements, or sound waves. Simulate the rippling movement of sound waves by performing the following:

- Slinky® Stretch: Have two students hold each end of an outstretched Slinky®. Ask one student to push one end of it up and down to send a wave to the other end.
- Marble Mash: Place six marbles close together in a line. Have a student roll another marble into the last marble in line. This will cause each marble to hit the one next to it and roll.
- Water Wave: Fill a 9" x 13" pan with 1½ inches of water. Place a small slip of paper on the surface of the water at one end of the pan. Have a student drop a penny into the water at the other end of the pan. Direct students to observe the ripples produced by the penny. The ripples will move the paper.
- Domino Dance: Set up a row of dominoes close together. Have a student push over the first domino. Direct your students to watch how the wave travels down the line of dominoes.

# Ears to Music!
## (Listening Skills, Classifying)

Soothe your students as they classify musical sounds with this listening activity. In advance, make a copy of page 20 for each child. Introduce your students to three categories of instruments (stringed, wind, percussion) by reading *Meet the Orchestra* by Ann Hayes (Harcourt Brace Jovanovich, Publishers; 1995). Explain to students that musical instruments use vibrations to make sounds. For example, the strings on a guitar vibrate when plucked, blowing air across the mouthpiece of a flute causes vibrations inside it, and striking a drum causes vibrations. Then ask your students to close their eyes and listen to a recording of instrumental music. Challenge students to name an instrument that produced a sound they remember hearing and record it on a class chart according to the three categories as shown. Then give each child a copy of page 20 and ask her to complete it by classifying the instruments, using the chart for reference.

# Instruments

| Stringed | Wind | Percussion |
|---|---|---|
| guitar | flute | drum |
| violin | clarinet | cymbals |
| | tuba | triangle |

## Traveling Sound
### (Experiment)

Hitch a ride on a sound wave with these sound-travel experiments. Tell students that sound travels through almost any substance and that they will experiment in small groups to see if sound travels better through a solid, a liquid, or a gas. To begin, have small groups sit at desks or tables. Give each group a new comb and a clear container filled with water. Have each group hypothesize about which medium (solid, liquid, or gas) sound will travel through best. Then ask one student in each group to strum the teeth of the comb with his thumb as the group listens. Next, have a different student strum the comb against the edge of the desk as another student listens by placing one ear on the desk. Finally, have one student strum the comb underwater as another student listens with one ear pressed against the container.

Ask each group to determine which experiment demonstrated sound traveling through a solid, a liquid, and a gas and then decide in which medium sound traveled best. Explain to your students that the more dense the substance is, the quicker sound will travel through it. Accordingly, sound travels faster through solids and liquids than it does through gases. So the sound produced by the comb and the desk should have produced the better sound.

## Quiet Please!
### (Critical Thinking)

Lower the noise level as your students conduct this calm critical-thinking activity. In advance, collect a windup clock and a variety of sound-absorbing material such as corrugated cardboard, carpet, and foam rubber. Explain to students that some materials are not good *conductors* of sound, therefore they provide insulation against noise. To begin, ask a student to place the clock on a table and set off the alarm while the group listens from a few feet away. Instruct a small group of students to experiment by covering the alarm clock with one material. Then have students listen to the alarm again from the same distance. Repeat the process until all materials have been tested. Then ask students to decide which material was the best sound insulator.

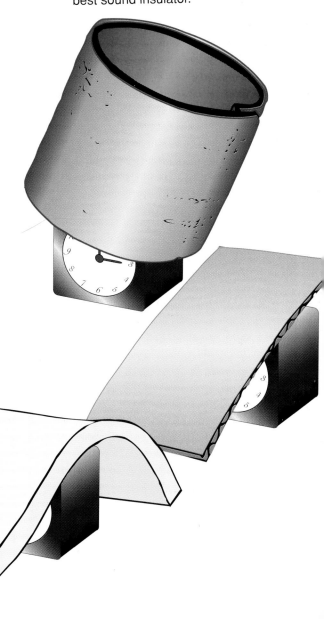

# Journey to the Center of the Ear
### *(Making a Booklet)*

Take your students down the path of a sound wave as it travels through the ear with this booklet-making activity. Tell students that sound waves enter the *outer ear,* vibrate through the *middle ear,* change into nerve signals in the *inner ear,* and are then sent to the brain and interpreted as sound. To illustrate this process, help each student follow the steps below to make a booklet.

**Materials for each student:**
1 copy of pages 22 and 23
1" square of aluminum foil
1" square of waxed paper
three ¹⁄₂" x 3" paper strips
scissors
glue
crayons

## Surround Sound
### *(Completing a Chart)*

Generate student awareness of how sound is measured with the following "sound-sational" activity. To begin, read aloud *Sounds All Around* by Wendy Pfeffer (HarperCollins Publishers, Inc.; 1999). Then explain to your students that *decibel* units ranging from 0 (the weakest sound humans can hear) to 160 (the threshold of pain begins at 140) are used to measure sound intensity. Give each child a copy of page 21 and ask him to color and then cut out the illustrations at the bottom of the page. Instruct him to use the information included on the chart to help him determine where to glue each cutout.

**Steps:**
1. Color and then cut out the booklet pages.
2. Cut apart the picture squares on the booklet cover and glue them in place.
3. Outer ear: Cut the two slits as indicated by the dotted lines on the page. Cut out the sound wave strip and slide it into the slits.
4. Middle ear: Cut out a one-inch waxed paper oval and glue it atop the oval labeled "eardrum." Then cut out the three patterns. Accordion-fold the three ¹⁄₂" x 3" paper strips, and then use each strip and glue to attach each pattern to the appropriate space on the booklet page.
5. Inner ear: Cut out the patterns and glue them in place. Cut a half-inch aluminum foil oval and then glue it atop the oval window.
6. Glue the pages together as indicated and accordion-fold to create a booklet.

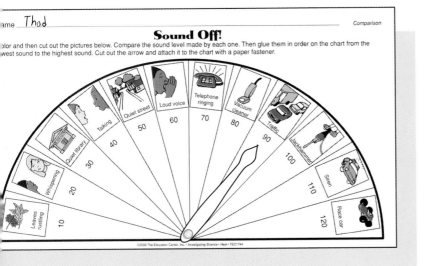

# Places Please!

Help the instruments find their places in the orchestra. Cut out the picture squares and then glue them in the correct instrumental section according to how each one makes sound.

**Percussion** instruments make sound when hit or shaken.
**Wind** instruments use air to make sound.
**Stringed** instruments make sound when strings vibrate.

Percussion

Strings

Conductor

Wind

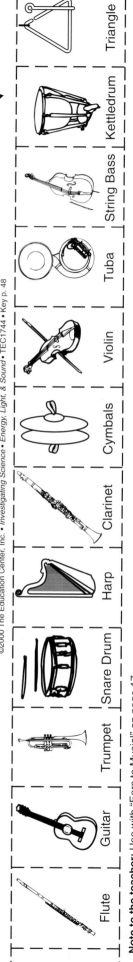

| Flute | Guitar | Trumpet | Snare Drum | Harp | Clarinet | Cymbals | Violin | Tuba | String Bass | Kettledrum | Triangle |

©2000 The Education Center, Inc. • *Investigating Science • Energy, Light, & Sound* • TEC1744 • Key p. 48

**Note to the teacher:** Use with "Ears to Music!" on page 17.

Name _____

# Sound Off!

Color and then cut out the pictures below. Compare the sound level made by each one. Then glue them in order on the chart from the lowest sound to the highest sound. Cut out the arrow and attach it to the chart with a paper fastener.

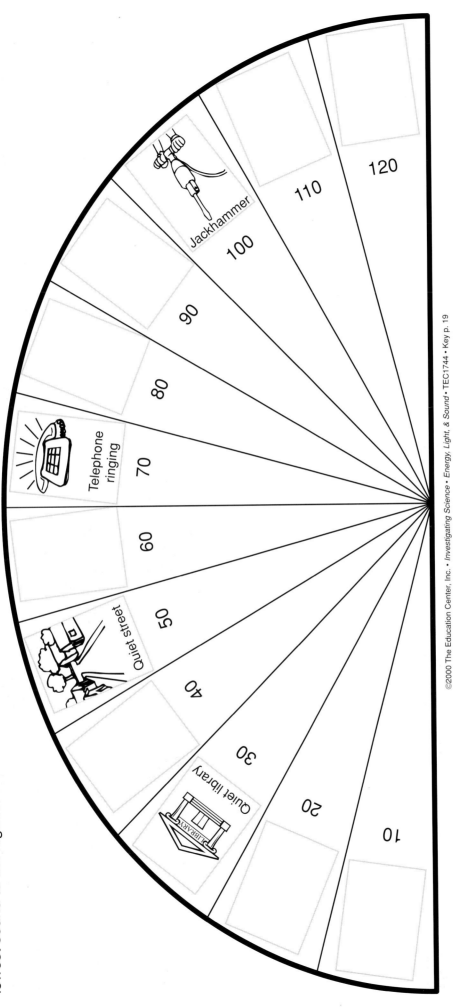

Jackhammer

120

110

100

90

80

Telephone ringing

70

60

Quiet street

50

40

30

Quiet library

20

10

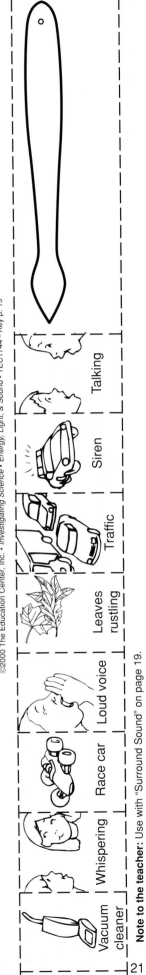

| Vacuum cleaner | Whispering | Race car | Loud voice | Leaves rustling | Traffic | Siren | Talking |

©2000 The Education Center, Inc. • *Investigating Science • Energy, Light, & Sound* • TEC1744 • Key p. 19

**Note to the teacher:** Use with "Surround Sound" on page 19.

21

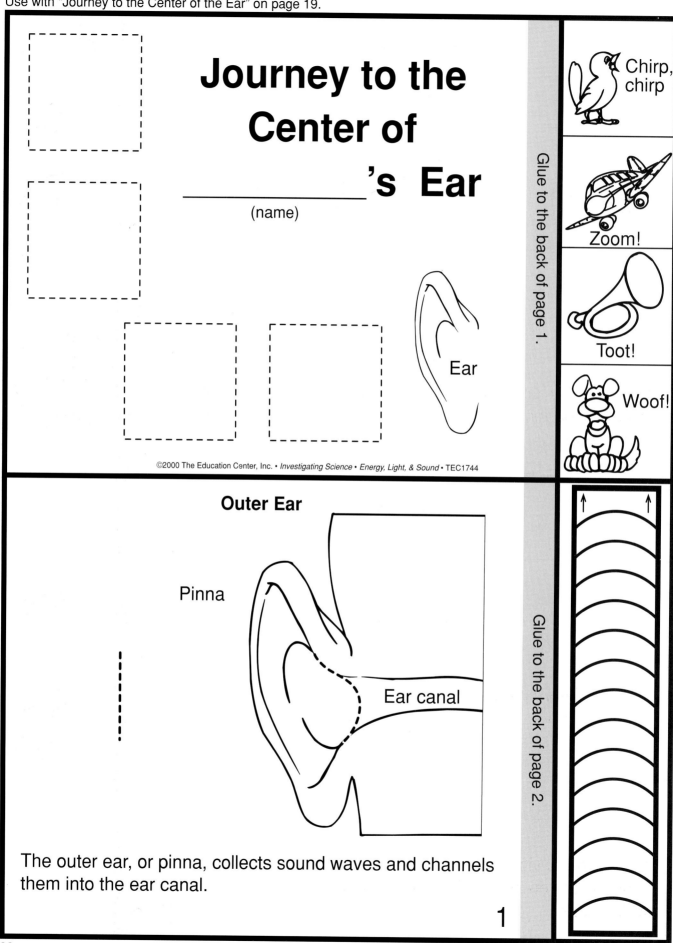

# Journey to the Center of

_____ 's Ear

(name)

Ear

Chirp, chirp

Zoom!

Toot!

Woof!

Glue to the back of page 1.

## Outer Ear

Pinna

Ear canal

Glue to the back of page 2.

The outer ear, or pinna, collects sound waves and channels them into the ear canal.

1

## Middle Ear

eardrum

hammer
(malleus)

anvil
(incus)

stirrup
(stapes)

Glue to the back of page 3.

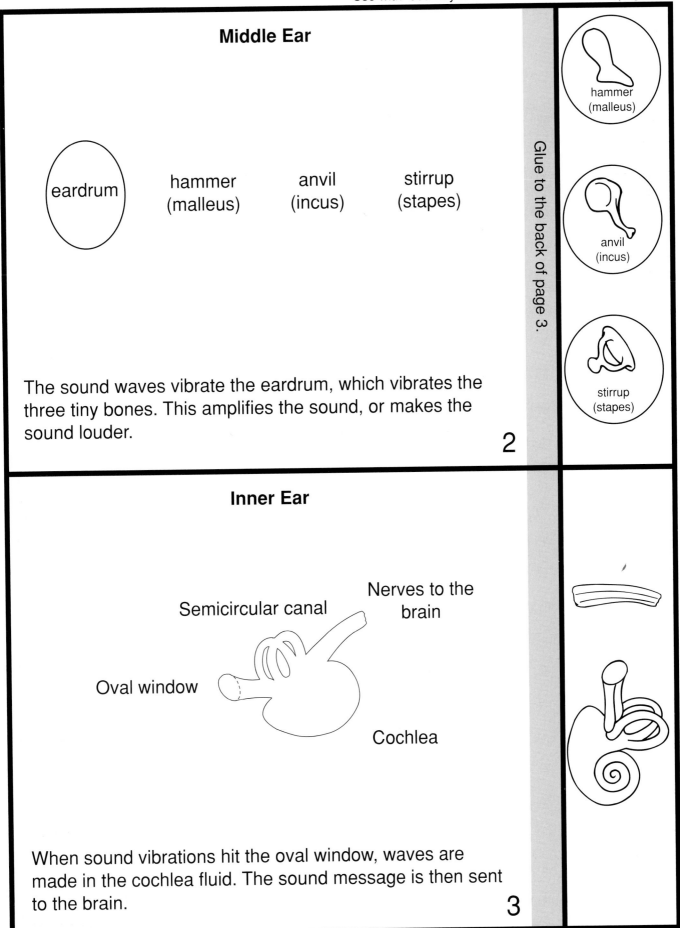

hammer
(malleus)

anvil
(incus)

stirrup
(stapes)

The sound waves vibrate the eardrum, which vibrates the three tiny bones. This amplifies the sound, or makes the sound louder.

2

## Inner Ear

Semicircular canal

Nerves to the
brain

Oval window

Cochlea

When sound vibrations hit the oval window, waves are made in the cochlea fluid. The sound message is then sent to the brain.

3

# Heat

*Warm up to the idea of learning about heat with these ideas and reproducibles. It's truly a hot subject!*

## Heat—a Hot Topic
### (Making a Mobile, Association)

Use this activity to introduce your students to the concept of heat and how it is produced. Explain to students that heat is a form of energy given off by a source. Further explain that heat on Earth is produced by six main sources: the Sun, Earth's interior, chemical reactions, nuclear energy, electricity, and friction. To help reinforce this information, have each student make a heat-source mobile. Distribute the materials listed below and follow the steps to complete the project. For a hot display, hang the completed mobiles from the ceiling in your classroom.

### Materials needed for each student:
1 white construction paper copy of pages 31 and 32
9" paper plate
6 lengths of string (8", 12", 16", 20", 24", 28")
1 length of string for hanging the mobile
scissors
glue
access to a hole puncher
crayons or markers
pushpin

### Steps:
1. Color and cut apart the mobile patterns and picture cards on pages 31 and 32. Match and glue each picture card to the appropriate mobile pattern.
2. Punch six equally spaced holes around the edge of the paper plate; then punch a hole in the top of each pattern where indicated.
3. Tie a different length of string to each hole around the plate, from shortest string to longest string. Then tie one pattern to the opposite end of each string as shown.
4. Use a pushpin to punch two small holes in the center of the plate.
5. Thread a length of string through the two holes; then tie the ends together.

## Warm Up With a Good Book

*Experiments With Heat* (A New True Book) by Walter Oleksy (Children's Press, 1986)
*Fun With Heat* (Simple Science) by Maria Gordon (Thomson Learning, 1995)
*The Magic School Bus® in the Arctic: A Book About Heat* by Joanna Cole (Scholastic Inc., 1998)

## Background for the Teacher

- *Heat* is a very important form of energy that people depend on for life.
- The molecules of a heated substance move quickly and take up more space, causing the substance to expand.
- A *heat source* is anything that gives off heat. Our most important source of heat is the Sun.
- Earth contains heat deep inside. Some of this heat escapes by way of *volcanoes* and *geysers.*
- *Friction* is a source of heat produced when one object rubs against another.
- *Nuclear energy* can produce great amounts of heat, which can be used to generate electricity.
- *Chemical reactions* produce heat by causing chemical changes.
- Heat travels in three ways: *radiation, convection,* and *conduction.*
- *Heat* and *temperature* are related but aren't the same. Temperature is a measure of the amount of internal energy an object has.
- *Insulation* controls the flow of heat by keeping it in or out of an area.
- A *thermometer* is an instrument used to measure temperature.

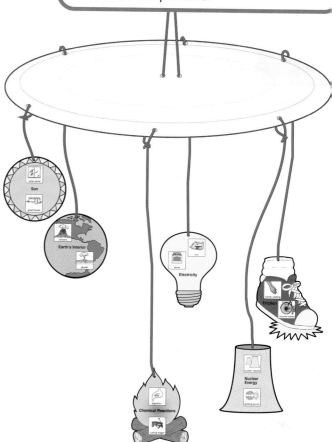

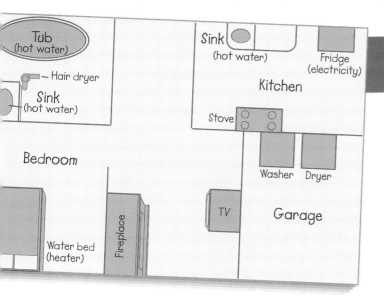

## Helpful Heat
### (Drawing and Labeling a Diagram)

Help your students become aware of the daily uses of heat in their homes with this simple activity. Distribute a blank sheet of paper to each child. Have the student use a pencil and ruler to sketch a layout of his home. Next, instruct him to draw and label objects in the house (oven, coffeepot, iron, fireplace, candle, etc.) that give off heat. Then have each child take his sketch home to compare it with the actual layout of the home. Ask him to add to his sketch any additional ways heat is used. Designate a day to return papers; then have students share the various ways heat is used in their homes. Display the sketches on a bulletin board titled "Helpful Heat in My Home."

## Molecules on the Move
### (Experiment, Scientific Process)

The race is on to find out whether the molecules of warm substances or cool substances move more quickly! Use this simple demonstration to show your youngsters that heat sets molecules in motion. To begin, divide the students into small groups. Then supply each group with the materials listed and guide each group through the steps shown. After completing the experiment, discuss the predictions and results with the class. *(The molecules of the hot water move much more quickly than the molecules of the cold water, therefore mixing the food coloring faster.)*

**Materials for each group:**
1 copy of page 33 per child
2 clear plastic cups
1 sheet of white paper
cold water
hot water
food coloring
crayons

**Steps:**
1. Fold the sheet of white paper in half to make a crease in the center. Unfold the paper and write "cold" on one half and "hot" on the other half.
2. Place one cup on each half of the paper.
3. Fill the cup on the side labeled "cold" two-thirds full with cold water. Fill the cup on the side labeled "hot" two-thirds full with hot water.
4. Predict what will happen when food coloring is dropped into each cup. Write your prediction on page 33; then draw a picture of your prediction.
5. Put one drop of food coloring in each cup. *(Do not stir the water.)*
6. Observe the drop of food coloring in each cup for three minutes.
7. Record the results of the experiment and then color the cups to show the results.
8. Fill in what you learned from the experiment in the conclusion section of page 33.

# Mighty Molecule Says
### (Game)

Have some fun with your students by combining "Simon Says" with moving like a molecule. Take students outdoors to a large play area. Direct students to spread out so that there's at least an arm's length between each student. Tell your students they are going to be molecules. Inform students that warm molecules move faster than cool molecules. Next, tell your students that they are going to play a game similar to Simon Says. Explain that they'll need to listen carefully as you read out commands (see list of suggested commands on this page). If the command refers to doing something involving heat, each molecule should run in place quickly. If the command refers to doing something that's cold, each molecule should run in place but in slow motion. Remind your students that they should only react to the command if they hear you say "Mighty Molecule says" before the command. Any students reacting to a command not given by Mighty Molecule have to step out of the game. Continue playing the game until one molecule remains.

Mighty Molecule says, "Roast marshmallows."

**Mighty Molecule says:**
sit next to a fireplace
freeze an ice cube
turn on a heater
cook dinner
roast marshmallows
drink a cold soda
use the microwave
take a hot bath
build a snowman
turn on the air conditioner

# Heat It Up!
### (Experiment)

Watch the temperature rise with this experiment that has students learning how chemical reactions create heat. Divide students into small groups. Gather the materials listed; then follow the steps to complete the experiment. After each group has completed the experiment, explain that the vinegar removed the protective coating on the steel wool, causing a chemical reaction known as rust. As the wool pad rusted, heat was released, making the temperature rise.

**Materials needed for each group:**
large jar with a lid
student thermometer (thermometer must fit inside the jar with the lid on)
half a soap-free steel wool pad
small amount of vinegar
dish
clock

**Steps:**
1. Seal the thermometer in the jar for five minutes; then remove the thermometer and quickly read the temperature.
2. Make a hole in the center of the steel wool pad (big enough for the end of the thermometer to fit in) with your thumbs; then soak the pad in vinegar in a dish for $1\frac{1}{2}$ minutes.
3. Squeeze out any excess vinegar from the pad and then place it in the bottom of the jar.
4. Insert the thermometer into the jar so that the bottom of the thermometer sits inside the hole of the steel wool pad; then tighten the lid.
5. Observe the thermometer and steel wool for five minutes; then read the thermometer again.

# Focus on Friction
### (Experiment, Art)

Why does the squeaky wheel always get the grease? When objects rub against each other, they produce friction. Friction is usually unwanted because it can cause damage. People apply lubricants to lessen friction. Experiment with friction by having each student rub her hands together until they feel hot. Explain to students that some of the energy used to rub their hands together changed into heat. Next, have each child apply a small amount of hand lotion and repeat the exercise. *(Please be aware of any student allergies.)* Have students discuss the difference the lotion made in rubbing their hands together. *(The hands slid across each other more easily, producing less friction.)* Then distribute a blank sheet of paper to each student before taking your class on a walk around your school campus. Direct youngsters to look for sources of friction around the school (shoes against the sidewalk, car tires against the pavement, sliding a book across a table, etc.) and draw a picture of the source of friction on their papers. Display the drawings on a bulletin board titled "Friction Finds."

# In the Bend With Friction
### (Experiment)

Friction not only occurs when two separate objects rub together, but also when the molecules within a single object rub together. Use this simple experiment to prove that friction can occur within an object. Distribute a large paper clip to each student. Have each child carefully bend a section of the paper clip back and forth six times. Then instruct him to feel the paper clip where it was bent. The paper clip will feel warm. Explain to students that the warmth felt was due to the molecules in the paper clip being rubbed against each other during the bending process. Have students repeat the process with different sections of the paper clip. After completion of the activity, collect and discard the paper clips.

## Solar Snack Recipes
**Note:** To insure the quickest cooking time, choose a very sunny day to heat solar oven snacks. Check the snacks often and eat them once they are heated.

### Solar S'mores
**Ingredients for one:**
1 graham cracker
1 square of chocolate
1 large marshmallow

**Directions:**
Break the graham cracker in half. Stack the chocolate square and then the marshmallow on one graham cracker half. Top with the second graham cracker half. Heat the s'more in the solar oven in the Sun for several hours. Delicious!

### Sunbeam Pizza
**Ingredients for one:**
$1/2$ English muffin
1 tbsp. pizza sauce
2 slices pepperoni
2 tbsp. mozzarella cheese

**Directions:**
Spread the pizza sauce on the English muffin. Top the muffin with pepperoni and then cheese. Heat in the solar oven for several hours. Yummy!

### Solar Chips 'n' Dip
**Ingredients for one serving:**
one 1" cube of Velveeta® cheese
1 tsp. mild salsa
1 serving corn chips

**Materials:**
paper cup
spoon

**Directions:**
Place the cheese in a small paper cup; then add the salsa. Put the cup and the corn chips in the solar oven. Heat the dip and chips for several hours. Stir the dip and enjoy!

# Solar Snacks
## (Making and Using a Solar Oven)

The Sun provides us with a great source of heat. Solar energy is a valuable resource consisting of heat, light, and other forms of electromagnetic radiation. Solar energy is captured and used to heat water, cool and heat buildings, produce electricity, and cook food. Help your youngsters understand how the Sun can cook food and satisfy a growling tummy in need of a snack by making solar ovens. Gather the materials listed below; then guide the students through the steps to complete and use their solar ovens (see recipes at right).

**Materials needed for each child:**
shoebox
aluminum foil
plastic wrap
tape

**Steps:**
1. Line the interior sides of the shoebox with aluminum foil (shiny side out).
2. Tape any overlapping aluminum foil to the outside of the box.
3. Follow one of the recipes shown to create a solar snack.
4. Place the prepared solar snack in the box.
5. Cover the top of the box with plastic wrap; then secure the edges with tape.
6. Place the solar oven in a safe sunny place outdoors. Leave the oven in the Sun for several hours.
7. Remove the solar snack and observe how the solar oven heated the snack.
8. Eat up!

## Spinning Spirals
*(Demonstration, Art)*

Art and science meet with this spiral decoration! Use the following activity to help your youngsters understand convection currents. In advance, duplicate page 34 to make a class set. Then gather the following supplies: one six-inch length of string per child and a lamp with a shade. Have each student decorate and cut out the spiral pattern along the bold lines. Help each student use his pencil to poke a small hole in the center of the spiral. Next, have the student tie a knot in the end of a length of string. Then have him thread the unknotted end of the string through the hole in the spiral, stopping once the knot reaches the hole.

Inform your students that they are going to use their spirals to prove that warm air rises from a heat source. Explain to your students that when cold air is heated, it rises and then cold air rushes in to replace it, creating a convection current. Place the lamp on the floor; then turn it on. While waiting for the air around the bulb to heat up, have each child hold his spiral by the string and watch for movement. (The spiral shouldn't rotate.) Then have a student volunteer hold his spiral above the hot bulb, making sure not to touch the paper against the bulb. Direct students to notice how the spiral begins to rotate. Have students discuss what's making the spiral spin. Guide students into understanding that the heated air around the bulb is rising, causing the paper spiral to rotate. Give each student an opportunity to hold his spiral above the hot bulb to watch it spin.

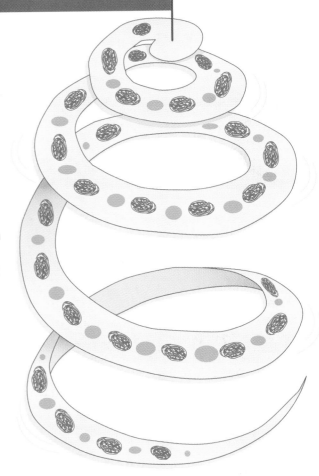

## Going Up?
*(Demonstration)*

Up, up, and away with heated air! This simple activity will prove to students that heated air rises. Explain to students that hot-air balloons rise when the cool air inside the balloon is heated. Next, demonstrate the activity by asking one child to hold a small trash can liner upside down while you use a hair dryer to blow warm air into the bag for approximately ten seconds. *After* the hair dryer has been turned off, instruct the child to let go of the bag. *(The warmed air inside the bag carries it upward.)*

To add a twist, use a hair dryer with cool and warm settings. After completing the first demonstration with the hair dryer blowing warm air into the bag, repeat the activity and set the hair dryer on the *cool* setting. Have students compare the results.

# Keep It Out!
## (Experiment)

Help your students learn how to keep the heat out with the following experiment. Explain to your students that heat flows from objects with higher temperatures to objects with lower temperatures when they are in contact. This presents a problem to people who want their homes cooler than the outside air in the summer. The solution is insulation. Explain that insulation is a way of controlling the flow of heat into or out of an area. Divide students into small groups. Gather the materials listed below; then follow the steps to have students discover which materials reduce the flow of heat.

**Materials needed for each group:**
5 ice cubes of the same size
piece of cloth
bubble wrap
aluminum foil
Styrofoam® cup
clock

### Steps:
1. Put one ice cube in the cup; then wrap one cube in the cloth, one in the bubble wrap, and one in the aluminum foil. Set the remaining ice cube aside to represent the control.
2. Record the starting time.
3. Observe the ice cubes, noting how long it takes each cube to turn to water.
4. Discuss which form of insulation worked the best in keeping the heat away from the ice cube. *(The Styrofoam cup is the most effective insulator. The aluminum foil is the least effective insulator.)* Then have students state the reason why the other insulators did not work as well. *(The heat moved through some materials more easily than others, making the ice cube melt faster.)*

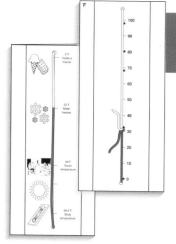

# The Ups and Downs of Heat
## (Making a Thermometer Model)

Use this activity to help students understand temperature measurement. Explain to students that a thermometer detects the amount of heat energy a substance has. Have each child make her own string thermometer to follow the temperature in your area. Distribute the materials listed; then guide each student through the steps shown to complete a thermometer model. After each student has constructed her thermometer, direct her to slide the string so the top of the red yarn is even with a star; then have her turn the thermometer over to see where the knot is located. The information near the knot explains the temperature reading.

For several days, have each student set her thermometer with the outdoor temperature. Appoint a student to check the thermometers. Then have students mark the day and temperature on the back of the thermometer near the knot.

**Materials needed for each student:**
tagboard copy of page 35
21" length of white yarn
scissors
red marker
access to a hole puncher

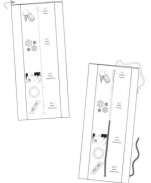

### Steps:
1. Cut along the dotted lines at the top and bottom of the thermometer pattern.
2. Fold along the center bold line.
3. Hole-punch the top and bottom of the pattern where indicated.
4. Fold the yarn in half. Then color *one-half* of the yarn with a red marker.
5. Thread the yarn through the holes and then match up the ends. Tie the ends in a knot. (Make sure there is no slack in the yarn and that it is not tied too tight.)

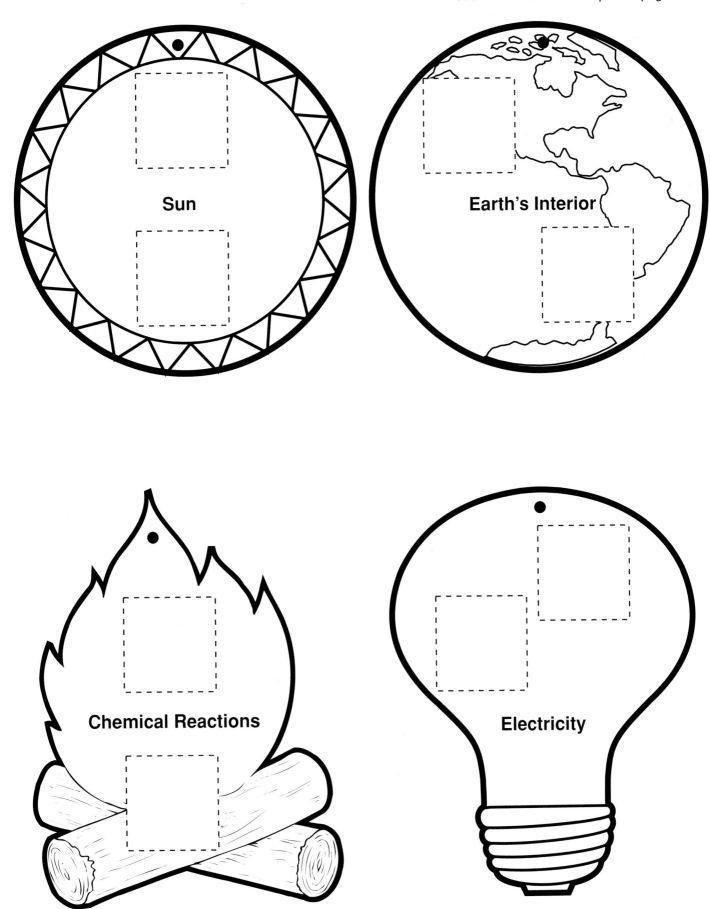

Sun

Earth's Interior

Chemical Reactions

Electricity

# Mobile Patterns

Use with "Heat—a Hot Topic" on page 24.

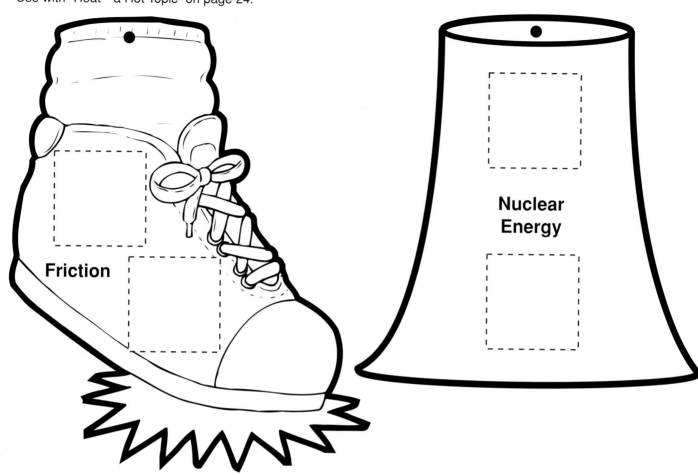

Friction

Nuclear Energy

# Picture Cards

Use with "Heat—a Hot Topic" on page 24.

| volcano | digestion | hands rubbing | nuclear reactor | solar panel | iron |
| splitting atoms | greenhouse | geyser | rusting wagon | stove | bicycle brakes |

# Molecules on the Move

**Prediction**—What I think will happen: _____

_____

**Results**—What happened: _____

_____

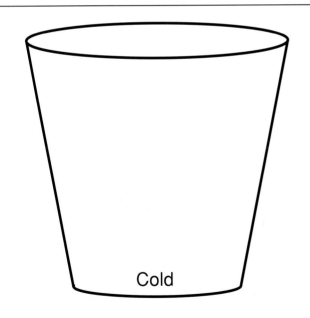

**Conclusion**—What I learned: _____

_____

# Pattern
Use with "Spinning Spirals" on page 29.

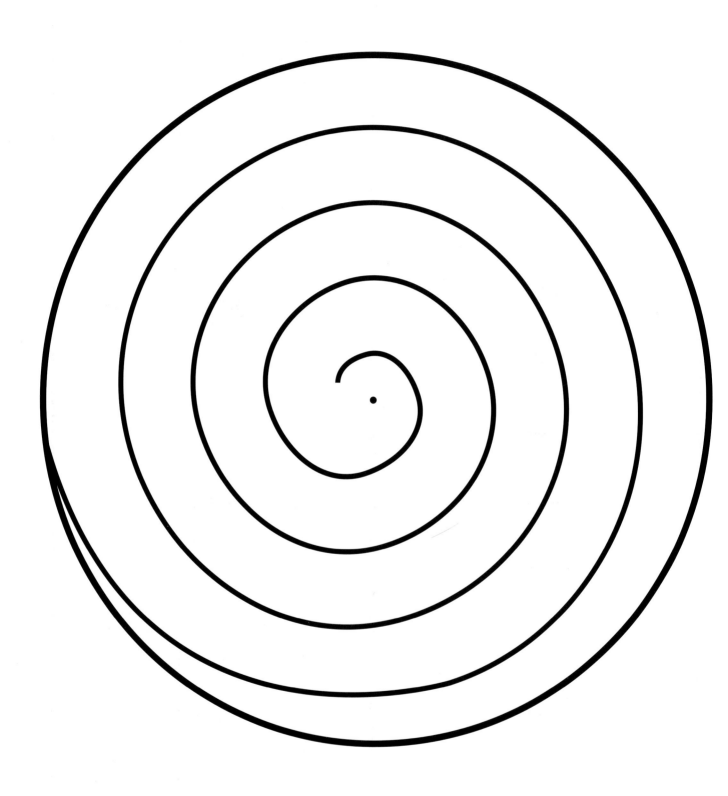

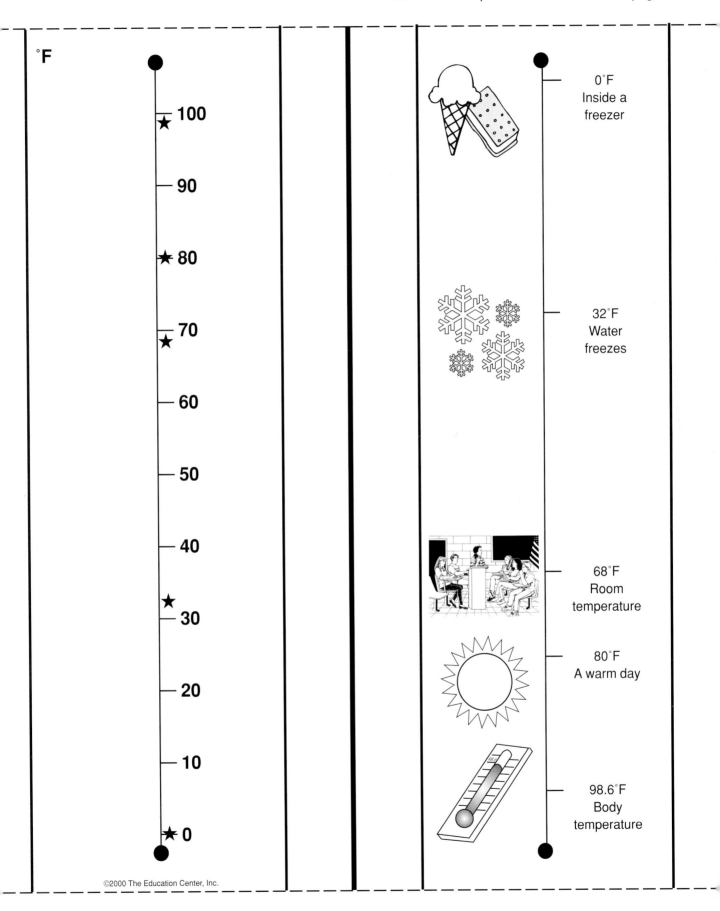

°F

★ 100
— 90
★ 80
★ 70
— 60
— 50
— 40
★ 30
— 20
— 10
★ 0

0°F
Inside a
freezer

32°F
Water
freezes

68°F
Room
temperature

80°F
A warm day

98.6°F
Body
temperature

©2000 The Education Center, Inc.

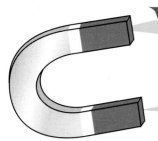

# Magnetism and Electricity

*Spark students' interest with this collection of fun magnetism and electricity activities!*

## Background for the Teacher

### Magnetism

- Magnets *attract,* or pull toward, items containing iron.
- Magnets are strongest at their ends, or *poles.* Magnets have north and south poles.
- The unlike poles of two magnets attract each other; the like poles *repel,* or push away, each other.
- A magnet's invisible force that attracts or repels is *magnetism.*

### Electricity

- Electricity is a form of energy that provides heat, light, and power.
- There are two forms of electricity: *static* and *current.*
- *Static electricity* jumps. Often it can be created by rubbing two objects together.
- *Current electricity* is electricity that flows. Most people use current electricity in their homes.
- A *circuit* is a complete path on which electricity travels.
- *Conductors* are materials that let electricity pass through them. *Insulators* are materials that do not let electricity pass through them.
- Power plants that burn fossil fuels (like oil and coal) produce most of our electricity. We continue to explore using alternative sources of electricity, such as solar, wind, and tidal energy.

## Making Magnets
### (Experiment, Listening Skills)

Draw your students' attention to the power of magnetism with this magnet-making activity. Break students into groups of four. Supply each group with a nail, a handful of paper clips, a magnet, and a copy of page 42. Then follow the directions shown to help each group create a magnet and test its strength.

### Teacher directions for using page 42:

1. Read aloud Steps 1 and 2. Allow time for each group to complete each task and answer the questions.
2. Explain to your students that not all the iron atoms in a nail are lined up; instead they are arranged randomly. When stroked with a magnet in one direction, the iron atoms align, temporarily making the object magnetic (see illustration). Temporary magnets do not keep their magnetic force. Further explain that a permanent magnet is made from steel or a mixture of iron, nickel, and cobalt. The iron atoms in a permanent magnet continue to stay aligned even when a magnetic field isn't present.
3. Ask each group to predict what will happen when the nail is rubbed ten more times.
4. Read aloud Steps 3 through 5. Allow time for each group to complete the tasks and answer the questions.
5. Have each group complete the illustration for Step 6.
6. Read aloud the Bonus Box; then have students suggest ways to demagnetize the nail.
7. Direct each group to test its ideas for demagnetizing the nail. *(To demagnetize a temporary magnet, tap it against a hard surface or run another magnet back and forth along it.)*

### Nail before stroking
Iron atoms unaligned and arranged in random order

### Nail after stroking
Iron atoms arranged in same direction in orderly pattern

## Electrifying Books

*Batteries, Bulbs, and Wires* (Young Discoverers) by David Glover (Kingfisher Books, 1993)

*Experiment With Magnets and Electricity* by Margaret Whalley (Lerner Publications Company, 1994)

*The Magic School Bus® and the Electric Field Trip* by Joanna Cole (Scholastic Inc., 1997)

*Science With Magnets* by Helen Edom (Usborne Publishing Limited, 1992)

*Understanding Electricity* (Science for Fun) by Gary Gibson (Copper Beech Books, 1995)

*What Makes a Magnet?* by Franklyn M. Branley (HarperCollins Children's Books, 199[

*Where Does Electricity Come From?* by C. Vance Cast (Barron's Educational Series, Inc.; 1992)

# Our Magnetic Hunt

## Magnetic Hunt
### (Experiment)

Send your students on a magnetism hunt to find out what types of things magnets attract. To begin, divide your youngsters into small groups. Provide each group with a magnet and eight to ten small magnetic and nonmagnetic items, such as paper clips, tacks, coins, keys, and rubber bands. Have each group predict which items they think are magnetic and which ones are nonmagnetic. Then instruct each group to use its magnet to sort the items into two groups: magnetic or nonmagnetic. Have the group compare the results with its predictions and then share the results with the class. Explain to your students that the items in the magnetic piles are attracted to the magnets because they contain iron. Next, challenge each group to test other items in the room or on the playground for magnetic attraction. After a designated time, gather the groups to share their findings. Draw a large horseshoe magnet pattern on a sheet of chart paper, and post it on the wall. Then, on the horseshoe, have your students write or draw pictures of the items they found to be attracted to the magnet. Next, have them write or draw pictures of the items they found that were not attracted to the magnet in the space around the pattern. Title the display "Our Magnetic Hunt."

## Magnet Races
### (Game)

Not only can magnets attract other magnets, but they can repel them too! Take this fun fact to the races. Break students into groups of four. Give each group four bar magnets. (Each racer will need two bar magnets.) Next, explain the rules of the game (shown in the box). Allow time for students to practice repelling one magnet with the other. To play, have each group stand at a table with two students on each side. Have the students on one side of the table race (repel) their magnets across the table. Then have the students on the other side race them back. Have the winners of each match race each other. Explain that the winner of that match is the group's winner. Hold a final match with the winners from each group racing against one another. And they're off!

### Rules for Magnet Racing
1. Place one magnet at the edge of the table.
2. Use a second magnet to repel the first magnet across the table to the other side. (Remember that like poles will repel.)
3. The first player to "push" his magnet to the opposite end of the table wins.

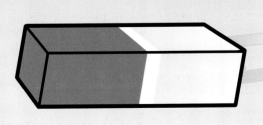

# Appreciating Electricity
## (Critical Thinking, Art, Writing)

Introduce your students to the world of electricity with this eye-opening activity. Instruct students to look around the classroom and identify objects that run on electricity. Next, tell them to think of electric objects that are used at home or in the community. List their thoughts on the board. Then challenge your students to imagine living without electricity. Ask them how life would be different at home, at school, and at play.

After discussing what life would be like with no electricity, give each student a sheet of drawing paper. Have her write and illustrate one way that her life would be different without electricity. Conclude the activity by inviting each student to share her work with the class. Then assemble the papers in a class book titled "Life Without Electricity."

# Safety First
## (Critical Thinking, Art, Oral Presentation)

Electricity can be lots of fun, but it can also be very dangerous. Have your students make public service announcements about electricity safety. Begin the lesson by discussing the dangers of electricity, such as electrical shock and lightning. Encourage students to share their ideas on staying safe around electricity. With your class, brainstorm a class list of electrical household hazards as well as hazards outside of the home. Then provide each student with one piece of tagboard on which to write and illustrate a rule for avoiding and/or preventing one of the listed hazards. When the posters are complete, schedule a visit with another class during which each of your students can share her safety knowledge. Then display the projects in the hallway for all to see…and learn!

# Ecstatic About Electricity
## *(Experiment)*

Invite students to discover something new about static electricity through this investigation. Before beginning, share "Static Electricity" below with the entire class. Then break students into groups of four. Supply each group with the materials listed. Challenge the members of each group to work together to complete the static electricity experiment on page 43. Instruct each group member to record the results of the experiment on his own chart. Finally, allow time for groups to share their results.

### Materials needed for each group:
2 inflated balloons on strings
1 piece of wool (a scarf or hat works well)
ten ¼" tissue paper squares
1 plastic ruler
1 copy of page 43 for each group member

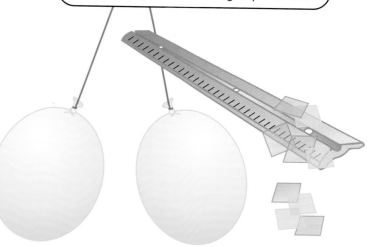

### Static Electricity
Sometimes a large amount of an object's atoms can lose or gain electrons, causing the whole object to take on an electric charge. *Static electricity* is a term used to describe an object that's carrying an electric charge. Two objects that have the same static electric charge repel each other. But two objects that have opposite electric charges will attract each other just like a magnet.

# From Generator to Lightbulb
## *(Reading Comprehension, Sequencing, Art)*

Show students how electricity is available in their homes by reading aloud *Switch On, Switch Off* by Melvin Berger (Thomas Y. Crowell Junior Books, 1989). Follow up the reading by guiding your students through the steps below to create a "television program" of a large community electric circuit. Then invite each student to take his project home for friends and family to view.

### Materials for each student:
1 copy of the reproducible on page 44
one 3" x 27" strip of paper
one 6" x 8½" piece of black construction paper
scissors
glue
crayons
ruler

### Steps:
1. Draw lines to divide the 27-inch strip of paper into nine three-inch sections.
2. In the second box on the strip, write the title "From Generator to Lightbulb."
3. Cut out the sentence boxes at the bottom of the reproducible.
4. Arrange them in order from first to last. (Check each student's arrangement before having her complete Step 5.)
5. Beginning with the third box, glue one sentence in each box of the paper strip.
6. Draw an illustration in the space above each sentence on the strip.
7. Write "by [your name]" in the last box on the strip.
8. Cut out the television from the reproducible.
9. Cut along the dotted lines inside the television.
10. Glue the back center portion of the television to the 6" x 8½" piece of construction paper.
11. Cut out the two black strips on page 44 and glue them to the television as antennae.
12. Thread the 27-inch strip of paper through the television slits.
13. View the program by slowly pulling the paper strip to the left.

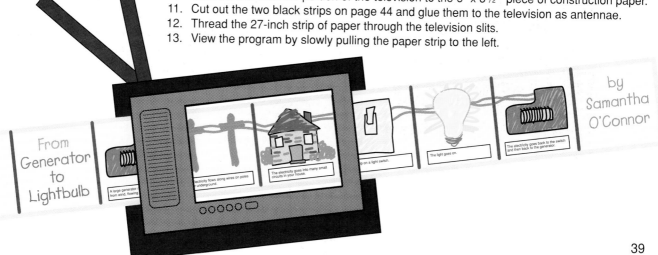

# Testing Conductors
## (Experiment, Sorting)

Help students better understand current electricity and the value of good conductors with the following fun experiment. In advance, follow the directions shown for making a test circuit for each group of four students in your class. Also supply each group with an assortment of household items: pencils, screws, keys, forks, paper clips. Then guide your youngsters through the steps below to investigate conductors and nonconductors of electricity.

**Steps:**
1. Explain that all circuits need an energy source, a conductor, and a *load* (the object using the electricity).
2. Give each group one preassembled test circuit. Instruct each group to examine its circuit. Explain that a circuit is a complete path around which electricity can flow. Ask each group to explain what is wrong with its test circuit. *(The circuit is not complete due to the break in the wire.)*
3. Remove the tape from one group's test circuit and show the class how the bulb lights when the two wires are connected. Retape the wires in their original positions.
4. Explain that each group is going to fix or complete its test circuit by placing various objects on the two exposed wires.
5. Further explain that if the bulb lights when the object is placed on the wires, then the object is a conductor of electricity. Have each group observe the intensity of the bulb's light with each test. Inform your students that some objects are better conductors of electricity than others and that some objects are not conductors.
6. Instruct each group to test each item, and then divide the items into three groups: good conductors, poor conductors, and nonconductors.
7. Have groups share their findings.

---

**Materials needed for each test circuit:**
one 6" x 9" piece of cardboard
1 C battery (1.5 volts)
three 3" plastic-coated wires with each
    end stripped to expose the wires
1 small bulb
1 small bulb holder
screwdriver
rubber band
tape

**Directions for making test circuit:**
1. Place the bulb holder on top of the 6" x 9" sheet of cardboard. Using a screwdriver, secure two wires to the bulb holder as shown.
2. Using a rubber band, attach one of the secured wires to the negative end of the battery.
3. Slide one end of the unsecured wire under the rubber band on the positive end of the battery as shown.
4. Tape all three wires down to the cardboard as shown. The free end of the wire attached to the positive end of the battery should be about a half-inch from the end of the wire attached to the bulb holder.

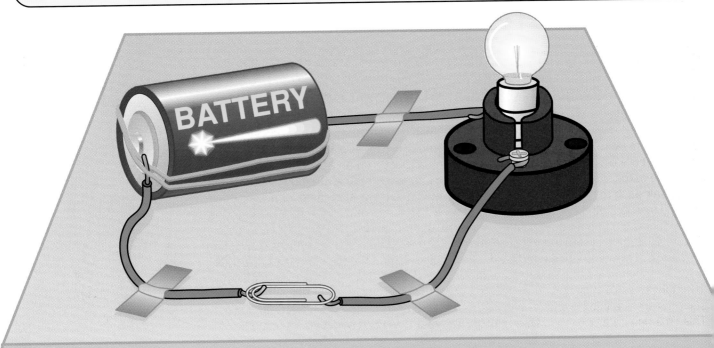

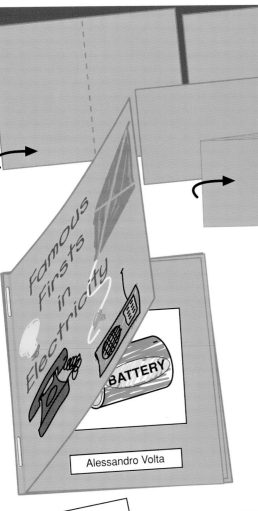

# Famous Firsts in Electricity

*(Listening Skills, Making a Booklet)*

Explore the early history of electric inventions with this book-making activity. Supply each student with a 9" x 12" sheet of construction paper, scissors, glue, crayons, and a copy of page 45. Then read aloud the steps shown to guide each student in making a "Famous Firsts in Electricity" booklet.

### Steps:
1. Fold the construction paper in half like a book. Cut along the fold to make two 9" x 6" pieces of paper.
2. Stack the two papers, fold them in half to create a 4½" x 6" booklet, and staple along the left-hand side as shown.
3. Cut out the picture cards and the name cards on page 45.
4. On the front of the booklet, write "Famous Firsts in Electricity."
5. Listen as your teacher reads the description of each person's discovery or invention. (See "Famous Firsts Facts" on this page.) Match each name with the correct picture.
6. Glue each picture card at the top of a separate booklet page. Then glue each corresponding name card at the bottom of each page.
7. Decorate the front cover and color the pictures.

---

**Famous Firsts Facts**
1. In 1752 Benjamin Franklin discovered lightning was electricity.
2. In 1800 Alessandro Volta made the first battery that produced a steady flow of electric current.
3. In 1831 Michael Faraday found that when he passed a magnet through a coil of copper wire, an electric current passed through the coil. This idea was later used to make electric generators and motors.
4. In 1876 Alexander Graham Bell invented the first telephone.
5. In 1879 Thomas Edison invented the lightbulb.
6. In 1888 Heinrich Hertz made the first radio transmission.

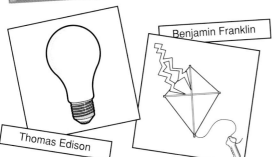

# Complete the Circuit

*(Listening Skills, Concepts Review)*

To culminate your study of magnetism and electricity, have your students play a game of "Complete the Circuit." The object of the game is to complete review questions without causing a break in the circuit with an incorrect answer. To set up the game, photocopy and cut out the cards (if desired, laminate them) on pages 46 and 47. Shuffle and deal out all the cards. A student can have more than one card. If there are more students than cards, pair each remaining student with one who has a card. Allow time for each student to become familiar with his card(s) and request help with pronunciations, if necessary. The game begins when a student stands, reads the bottom portion of his card, and sits down. The other students listen to the description. Then the student who has the matching term on the top of his card stands and reads the answer. After he reads the answer, he then reads the description on the bottom of the card and sits down. The game continues in this manner until the answer from the first card is read. The circuit is complete—but your students are likely to be charged for another round! Shuffle the deck and begin again. This time use a stopwatch to time how quickly your class can complete the circuit!

# Making a Magnet

> **Directions:**
> Complete each step as your teacher reads it aloud.
> Record your answers.

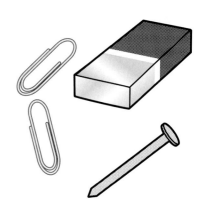

**Steps:**

1. Touch the nail to the paper clips. How many paper clips did it pick up? _____

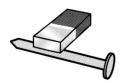

2. Rub the magnet on the nail ten times in one direction only. Touch the nail to the paper clips. How many paper clips did it pick up? _____

3. Repeat Step 2. How many paper clips did the nail pick up?

   _____

4. Repeat Step 2 again. How many paper clips did the nail pick up?

   _____

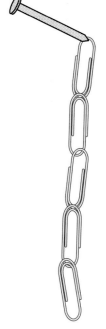

5. Did rubbing the nail more times increase the strength of the magnet? _____

6. Draw the particles in each nail.

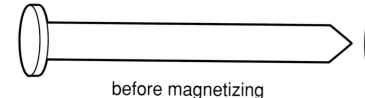

before magnetizing                    after magnetizing

> **Bonus Box:** How might you make the nail *not* a magnet again? Write your answer on the back of the page.

Name _____

# Ecstatic About Electricity

| What to Do | What Do You See? | Attract or Repel? | Why? |
|---|---|---|---|
| 1. Rub one balloon against the piece of wool. Hold the balloon against the wall and let go. | | | |
| 2. Rub each balloon against the piece of wool. Then hold the two balloons next to each other by the strings. | | | |
| 3. Rub your hair with the piece of wool ten times. On the last rub, slowly pull the wool away from your head. | | | |
| 4. Lay the paper squares on the table. Rub the ruler ten times with the wool. Slowly pass the ruler over the paper. | | | |

**Bonus Box:** Where else have you seen static electricity? Write your answer on the back of this page.

©2000 The Education Center, Inc. • *Investigating Science • Energy, Light, & Sound* • TEC1744

43

**Note to the teacher:** Use with "Ecstatic About Electricity" on page 39.

# Television Pattern and Sentence Boxes

Use with "From Generator to Lightbulb" on page 39.

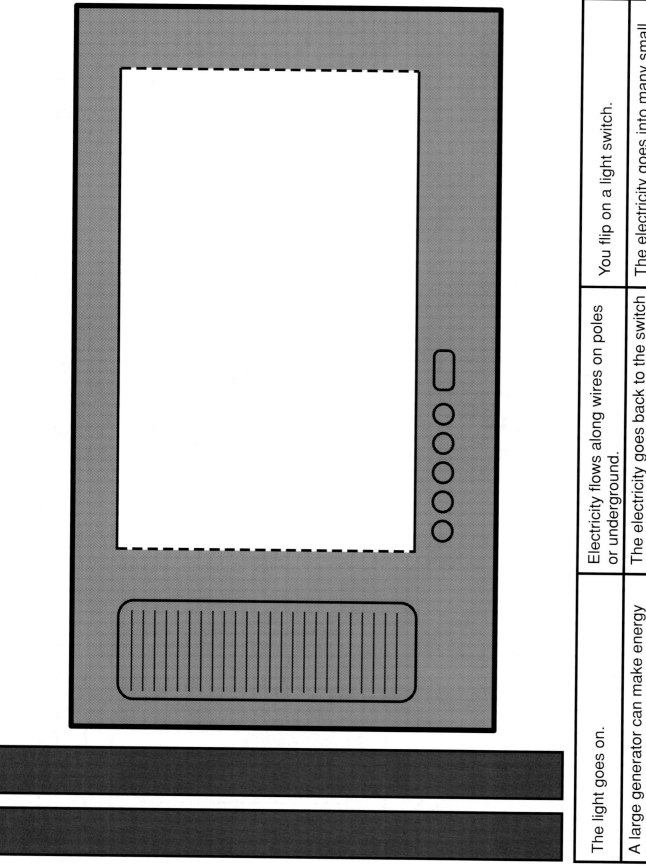

You flip on a light switch.

The electricity goes into many small circuits in your house.

Electricity flows along wires on poles or underground.

The electricity goes back to the switch and then back to the generator.

The light goes on.

A large generator can make energy from wind, flowing water, or steam.

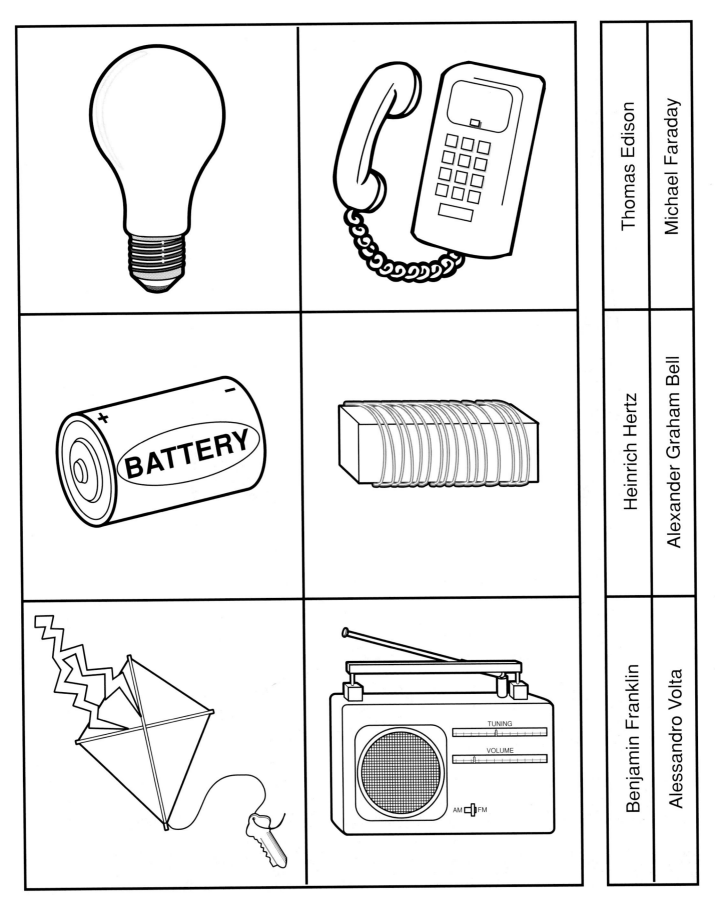

| | | Thomas Edison | Michael Faraday |
| | | Heinrich Hertz | Alexander Graham Bell |
| | | Benjamin Franklin | Alessandro Volta |

# Cards

Use with "Complete the Circuit" on page 41.

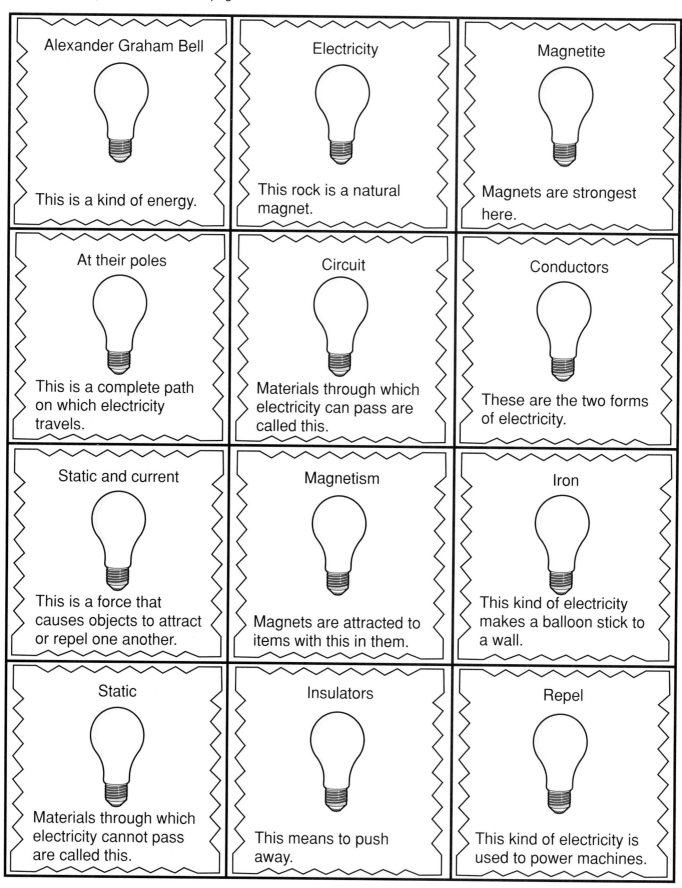

Alexander Graham Bell

This is a kind of energy.

Electricity

This rock is a natural magnet.

Magnetite

Magnets are strongest here.

At their poles

This is a complete path on which electricity travels.

Circuit

Materials through which electricity can pass are called this.

Conductors

These are the two forms of electricity.

Static and current

This is a force that causes objects to attract or repel one another.

Magnetism

Magnets are attracted to items with this in them.

Iron

This kind of electricity makes a balloon stick to a wall.

Static

Materials through which electricity cannot pass are called this.

Insulators

This means to push away.

Repel

This kind of electricity is used to power machines.

# Cards

Use with "Complete the Circuit" on page 41.

Current

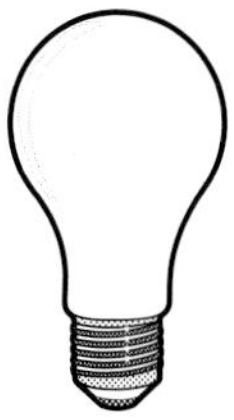

These can power generators.

Wind, flowing water, and steam

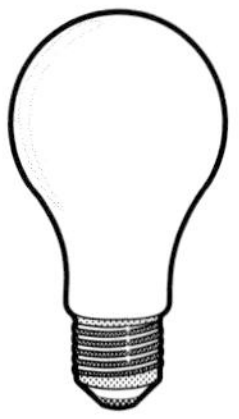

Opposite ends of magnets do this.

Attract each other

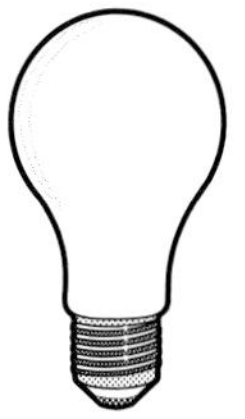

This is a giant magnet.

The earth

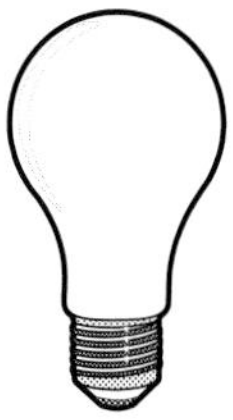

These are powered by current electricity.

A television, a lightbulb, and a computer

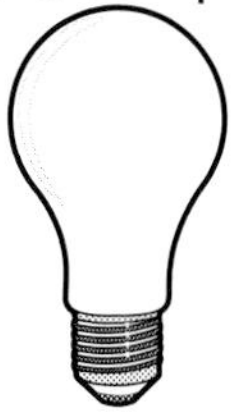

He discovered lightning is electricity.

Benjamin Franklin

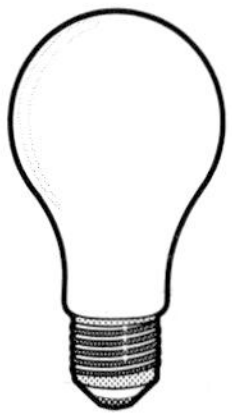

This object uses chemicals to make electricity.

A battery

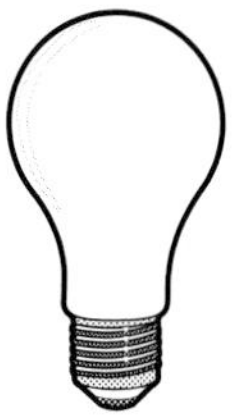

He invented the first lightbulb.

Thomas Edison

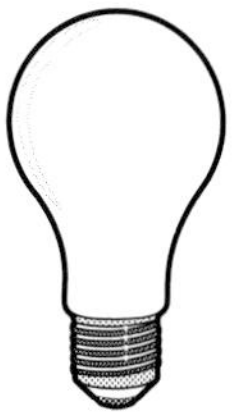

This machine makes electricity.

Generator

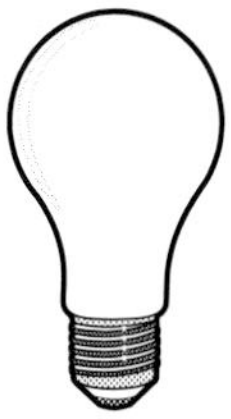

These magnetic poles repel each other.

Like poles

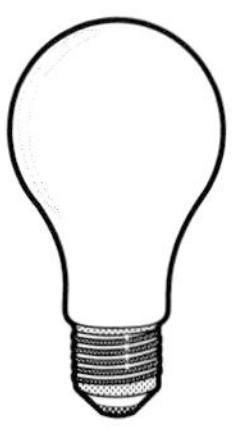

Electricity gives us these three things.

Heat, light, and power

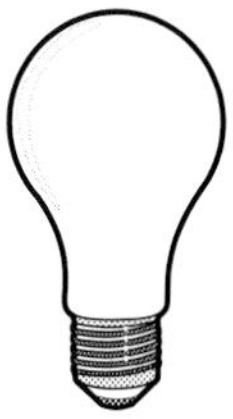

You complete a circuit when you turn this on.

A light switch

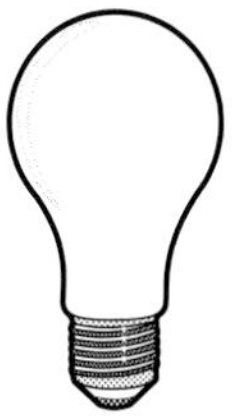

He invented the telephone.

# Answer Keys

**Page 20**

Wind Instruments:
Flute
Trumpet
Clarinet
Tuba

Percussion Instruments:
Snare Drum
Cymbals
Kettledrum
Triangle

Stringed Instruments:
Guitar
Harp
Violin
String Bass

**Pages 31–32**

Sun—solar panel, greenhouse
Earth's Interior—volcano, geyser
Chemical Reactions—digestion, rusting wagon
Electricity—iron, stove
Friction—hands rubbing, bicycle brakes
Nuclear Energy—nuclear reactor, splitting atoms

**Page 44**

Text boxes are in the following order:
Box 3: A large generator can make energy from wind, flowing water, or steam.
Box 4: Electricity flows along wires on poles or underground.
Box 5: The electricity goes into many small circuits in your house.
Box 6: You flip on a light switch.
Box 7: The light goes on.
Box 8: The electricity goes back to the switch and then back to the generator.

**Pages 46–47**

This is a kind of energy./Electricity
This rock is a natural magnet./Magnetite
Magnets are strongest here./At their poles
This is a complete path on which electricity travels./Circu
Materials through which electricity can pass are called this./Conductors
These are the two forms of electricity./Static and current
This is a force that causes objects to attract or repel one another./Magnetism
Magnets are attracted to items with this in them./Iron
This kind of electricity makes a balloon stick to a wall./Static
Materials through which electricity cannot pass are called this./Insulators
This means to push away./Repel
This kind of electricity is used to power machines./Curren
These can power generators./Wind, flowing water, and steam
Opposite ends of magnets do this./Attract each other
This is a giant magnet./The earth
These are powered by current electricity./A television, a lightbulb, and a computer
He discovered lightning is electricity./Benjamin Franklin
This object uses chemicals to make electricity./A battery
He invented the first lightbulb./Thomas Edison
This machine makes electricity./Generator
These magnetic poles repel each other./Like poles
Electricity gives us these three things./Heat, light, and power
You complete a circuit when you turn this on./A light switch
He invented the telephone./Alexander Graham Bell